From the authors

In 1983, my parents bought me a Sinclair ZX Spectrum and some games for my birthday. This began a phase that lasted nearly five years. Little did I know that nearly two decades later my interest in video games would return – but this time professionally, in my role as a teacher of English as a foreign language.

For 20 years or so, my relationship with video gaming and play would be a casual one. I occasionally played the popular PC games *Lemmings* or *Mine Sweeper*, and played *Mario Bros* with friends, nieces and nephews when the opportunity arose. However, I very much thought my gaming days were over. I did, however, return to playing video games briefly at the beginning of my teaching career. As an end-of-the-week activity, I would walk down to an internet café with several colleagues, connect to the same online 'first person shooter' game and spend happy hours blasting away at my fellow teachers. Then each of us moved on from that language school, I stopped playing and, for five years, gaming was gone.

It all changed one day in a computer room while teaching a secondary-level English class. We were in the middle of project work using Microsoft PowerPoint when a pair of fast finishers asked if they could play an online game. My interest was piqued: 'You can play the game if you tell me about it.' I can't remember much about the game itself but, listening to the two learners, I was surprised by their enthusiasm and fluency when talking about it. I began to see that there was something here for English language teaching.

That evening at home, I played a few other online games and, before long, a whole new world was opening up before my eyes. By playing online games and wearing my (virtual) teacher's hat, I began to see the language potential. At first it was simply describing instructions, but that soon moved on to describing the story, as I found games that were more narratively complex. Soon I turned to forums and fansites to help me complete the games.

Research had never been such fun!

Since then, I have started a wiki, archiving the best games, and co-run the *Digital Play* blog with Graham, posting lesson plans, activities and ideas for language teachers. I have also run numerous in-house training sessions, presented at conferences and written online articles, all concerned with using video games as language learning tools.

Computer gaming has always been a very social activity for me. As a teenager, I remember playing games such as *Space Invaders*, *Galaxia*, *Defender* and *Jump Bug* with friends in arcades, and at home playing with my brother on his Sinclair Spectrum. When the first 'text adventure' games started to appear, playing was always a collaborative effort with friends, helping each other solve the puzzles together.

After university, I remember playing computer games at lunchtimes with work colleagues. At one architectural practice I worked at, everyone would jump into a plane at the end of the day for a team game of *Flight Simulator*, and instructions for team members would echo around the two floors of the building.

Then, about 15 years ago, just after I'd started teaching, one of the other teachers at a summer school brought in a games console and set it up in our staffroom. As we played, some of the kids started hanging out on the balcony that overlooked the staffroom and shouted instructions to us on how to play the original *Tomb Raider* game. It was my first experience of games being used to generate language. I have since dabbled in using games with learners ever since, occasionally bringing my own PlayStation 3 into class for fun end-of-term karaoke and quiz-game sessions.

The Eureka! moment came for me one day in our computer room after playing part of an online game with my young learners. I had been reading out help from a 'walkthrough' (the written instructions on how to complete the game) and at the end of the class the learners asked me for a copy of the 12-page document. This was so they could carry on playing the game at home and finish it. This they did – without even realising they were enjoying English reading practice.

I realised there and then that games could be a powerful teaching and learning tool.

Finding out that Kyle had a similar interest was like finding a brother-in-arms. Soon we were brainstorming and sharing ideas of how best to use games with our learners, and then we worked together in the virtual world Second Life creating our own language learning quest games.

During this time, we had the idea of putting all we had discovered in a blog (*Digital Play*) and took the logical step of writing a book for teachers. I'm very happy to say, here it is!

Kyle

Graham

3

Contents

DELTA TEACHER DEVELOPMENT SERIES

Series editors Mike Burghall and Lindsay Clandfield

Digital Play

Computer games and language aims

Kyle Mawer and Graham Stanley

Published by
DELTA PUBLISHING
Quince Cottage
Hoe Lane
Peaslake
Surrey GU5 9SW
England

www.deltapublishing.co.uk

© Delta Publishing 2011

First published 2011

ISBN 978-1-905085-55-2

Edited by Mike Burghall
Designed by Christine Cox
Cover photo © Sandy MacKenzie/Shutterstock.com
Printed in the United Kingdom by TJ International

The many links in *Digital Play* were correct at the time of
going to press, but the Web is dynamic and changeable.
For updates and further links see *www.digitalplay.info/blog*.

Please note that inclusion in the book does not necessarily
mean that the authors or publishers of *Digital Play* endorse
all the websites or their content.

Acknowledgements

The authors would like to thank everyone we've had contact
with who has encouraged our pursuit of learning through
gaming. This includes the many teachers we have had the
pleasure to work with; all the learners who play-tested
activities; the directors of study who have had faith in us
and encouraged our digital dreams; our personal learning
network of friends and colleagues online; and our fellow
gamers in the G6 (BK, Pedro, Pershy, Turq) for all the fun,
games and banter on the boards. It has been your input,
feedback, ideas and enthusiasm that has helped us to learn
and to develop as edugamers.

A very special thank you goes to our editors Mike and
Lindsay, and to Nick, Christine, Helen and the rest of
the team at Delta, for your belief in us, encouragement,
enthusiasm and commitment to this project.

Kyle dedicates this book to vague beginnings, Ray guns and
lost Pegs and for times when the sun smells too loud.

Graham dedicates the book to Isabel for the smiles that win,
the tints that glow and all that's best of dark and bright.

Contents

5

'Play is the answer to how anything new comes about.'

Jean Piaget

Play, Dreams and Imitation in Childhood

Digital play

Children need to play. It is the part of their world which helps develop their communication, understanding and imagination. In spite of this, the role of play and games has not been central to school education. Instead, it is programmed activities and work that fill up the school day – and terms such as 'edutainment' cause some educators to shudder when they hear them mentioned. But should it be that way? We think not. Let us consider some of the following observations:

- *'Games are a more natural way to learn than traditional classrooms. Not only have humans been learning by playing games since the beginning of our species, but intelligent animals have as well.'* [1]
- *'The starkly obvious difference between games and traditional schooling is that good games always involve play, and schooling rarely does.'* [2]
- *'The question 'Can games have educational value?' becomes absurd. It is not games but schools that are the newfangled notion, the untested fad, the violator of tradition. Game-playing is a vital educational function for any creature capable of learning.'* [3]

It's not just about children, either. Play can make learning more productive and pleasurable for adults too. Playfulness helps us be more flexible, creative and resilient – and is a great source of happiness.

Play, then, yes – but why *digital* play?

For many 21st century learners, digital play is what now dominates their free time. Not only do they play computer games, but they spend much of their time talking about them with friends. And they also learn from them:

- *'Kids learn more positive, useful things for their future from video games than they learn in school.'* [4]
- *'The theory of learning in good video games fits better with the modern, high-tech, global world today's children and teenagers live in than do the theories (and practices) of learning that they see in school.'* [5]
- *'Computer and video games make it possible for students to learn to think in innovative and creative ways just as innovators in the real world learn to think creatively.'* [6]

For many 21st century teachers, whether teaching children or adults, introducing an element of digital play into your classrooms can open a doorway to a new way of learning – one that will better connect you to your learners, strengthen the sense of community, and bring more imagination, curiosity and fun to your classes.

The authors use the terms 'computer game', 'digital game' and 'video game' interchangeably: we consider these to be any type of interactive entertainment software, including games played on computers, game consoles and handheld devices.

Computer games and society

'It is curious that as parents, we'll insist that kids be given the time to play because it's important to childhood, but that work is deemed far more important later in life. I think work and play aren't all that different, to be honest.'
Ralph Koster [7]

In recent years, computer games have moved out of the margins of society and entered the mainstream of popular culture. In the wake of this, former distinctions between those people who play (male; teenagers) and those who don't (female; older generations) are now outmoded, although this idea still lingers in the minds of many people, including teachers, especially if they are divorced from the world of digital games.

There are few people, however, who are not now aware that much has changed with computer games. The rapid advances in the computer games industry have meant that it is fast becoming one of the most important sectors in the entertainment industry. And interestingly for anyone involved in education, game designers are now linking gameplay with learning in commercial games.

To see this, one only has to look at the popularity of 'casual' games (those targeted at a mass audience of people who don't normally play games) such as *Farmville*, now found in social networks like Facebook; games aimed at improving our IQ, such as Nintendo's *Brain Age*; or the adaptation of TV quiz programmes (eg *Who wants to be a millionaire?*) that test our general knowledge. There are even specially written language learning games (eg Sony's *Play English*, for the PSP) that offer a completely new way of self-study for those who want it.

This proliferation of games of all types shows that digital games now take many forms and have opened up many new audiences, covering different age groups and appealing to people of very different backgrounds than was the case before.

Nevertheless, despite these changes, many people still hold views that are proving to be stumbling blocks to computer games being more widely adopted and their educational potential appreciated. Perhaps the greatest bugbear of them all is the long-standing association that games have had with violence.

Violence

'Modern media, including video games, offer a vast library of imagery. But the intent to commit violence in the first place is not caused by that imagery.'
Steven Poole [8]

If you take at face value what you read about computer games in newspapers and most of what you hear about them on TV, you would believe the relationship between violent computer games and aggressive behaviour is clear: playing violent computer games triggers real-world violence. However, Lawrence Kutner and Cheryl K Olson, in the first in-depth study on the subject, conclude:

'Much of the information in the popular press about the effects of violent games is wrong … The strong link between video game violence and real world violence, and the conclusion that video games lead to social isolation and poor interpersonal skills, are drawn from bad or irrelevant research, muddleheaded thinking and unfounded simplistic news reports.' [9]

The main conclusion drawn from reading their book is that parents and teachers should relax. Concern is understandable, given the sensationalist news reports, but these concerns are no different from the unfounded worries previous generations had about the new media of their day. Although the arguments against games keep resurfacing from time to time, there is now a growing number of voices in favour of games, as mentioned in a recent report published by the MacArthur Foundation: *'Advocates of video games' potential … call attention to the 'tremendous educative power' of games to integrate thinking, social interaction and technology into the learning experience.'* [10]

Stereotypes

'40 per cent of all US video game players are women.'
Tom Chatfield [11]

Computer games are played by kids and teenagers, right? How many people do you know that still think this? And when many people think of computer games, an image pops into their head of a teenage boy alone in his bedroom, eyes glued to the screen while he destroys the ever-increasing onslaught of monsters storming towards him. Referring to a recent report on gaming in the UK, Diane Carr states:

'The figures show that more males play than females, but only in certain countries, and not in all genres, and that the average age of British female gamers is 30–35 years old. They represent 27.2% of UK gamers [and on] average they spend 7.2 hours per week playing games.' [12]

As these figures show, women and girls do play games. The statistics are clear: it is a mistake to associate computer gaming only with children or teenagers. Despite this, games still remain *'the preserve of adolescent boys'* [13] in the public imagination.

And the gap of understanding between those who play games and those who don't is starting to have a negative effect on society. Casas [14] has identified research that shows disruption to parental communication with their children *'as a result of their own insufficient understanding of, and unwillingness to take part in, game cultures which appear to captivate this new generation'.*

An equally popular view also holds that playing games is an anti-social activity, when the opposite is often true. Most people play computer games in the company of others, not to mention all of the activity that occurs outside the game (discussions about computer games with friends, etc). As Schott and Kambouri have found, *'recent research strongly refutes the popular idea that gameplaying is an antisocial activity'.* [15]

Computer games and education

On the whole, our educational systems have been slow to respond to the changes that are rippling through society. Many schools are still shackled to a 19th century factory model of education, with pupils sitting in rows with textbooks all open on the same page and facing both a blackboard (or whiteboard if a teacher is lucky!) and a teacher who directs the class from his or her position as 'sage on the stage'.

Of course, this is an exaggeration – especially when it comes to the language classroom. Many teachers have transformed their classrooms into learner-centred environments, where group- and pairwork is the norm and where learners use a wide variety of communicative materials and are often involved in project work.

> 'If the principles of learning in good video games are good, then better theories of learning are embedded in the video games many children play than in the schools they attend.'
> James Paul Gee [16]

However, many learners pass through the existing education system with more than just a feeling that it offers little of relevance to the 21st century world they live in. This needs to change. Ultimately, inspiring our learners and equipping them for the world outside the four walls of the classroom is what every teacher should be doing.

🔘 Revolution

The changes we refer to as rippling through society are those of the digital revolution – but having access to technology in the classroom is not a necessary part of this. Far more important is getting to know the students, finding out what they are interested in and discovering how they use or think they will use the language they are learning. We do believe, though, that in many cases you will find that your learners are already using a second language as part of their digital life outside of the classroom. It may be they are using the second language in ways that you hadn't ever considered.

> 'Today's students are no longer the people our education system was designed to teach.'
> Marc Prensky [17]

This generational 'digital divide' was first described by Marc Prensky, who labelled the new generation of connected, digitally-savvy students 'digital natives'. The average graduate, he said, would have *'spent less than 5,000 hours of their lives reading, but over 10,000 hours playing video games (not to mention 20,000 hours watching TV)'.* [18]

To some, the task of teaching this new generation of digital natives seems to be rather overwhelming, and John Palfrey and Urs Gasser speak for many of us when they say that *'teachers worry that they are out of step with the digital natives they are teaching, that the skills they have imparted over time are becoming either lost or obsolete, and that the pedagogy of our educational system cannot keep up with the changes in the digital landscape'.* [19]

This is one reason why the digital revolution *will* change education. It is already starting to have an impact in many of our organisations and schools. If you are one of the lucky teachers who have now started to see technology enter your classroom, you may have access to a computer and a data projector, or even an interactive whiteboard. If you are *very* fortunate, you will be teaching in a connected classroom (ie with an internet connection too) or you could have access to a computer room or have a classroom set of laptops at your disposal.

As access to digital technology increases in the classroom, demand for training, software, digital materials, websites and other resources to enhance both the learning and teaching experience is increasing. Using computer games can also be part of this.

Whatever your teaching situation is, though, it is essential to remember that it isn't *what* you have but what you *do* with what you have that is important. Bearing this in mind, we decided there should be something in *Digital Play* of value to teachers in all of the situations listed above.

Innovation

The idea of using computer games for training and education is not new. For many years, the term 'serious game' has been used to refer to a game designed for a purpose other than pure entertainment, and serious games have been developed for use in defence, health care, city planning and scientific exploration, to name but a few. The main aim of these games has been to train, investigate, simulate or advertise, and they are, more often than not, problem-solving games. The main advantage of many of these games has been financial, allowing processes and events to be simulated at a fraction of what it would normally cost.

The development and deployment of serious games has slowly helped computer games become more accepted in different sectors of society. Recently, things have taken a new turn, and a new wave of commercial computer games is starting to inspire educational innovation. One thing helping this is the increase in sophistication of top-of-the-range computer games (especially ones played on modern game consoles).

These new digital games have attracted the attention of educators who previously weren't interested. This is because it is evident to even a casual observer that many of these new games require hours of sustained concentration in order to complete them. As the games became more sophisticated, researchers such as James Paul Gee started to notice that computer games were also embodying good learning principles: *'Well, it turns out that the theory of learning in good video games is close to what I believe are the best theories of learning in cognitive science ... .'* [21]

This type of observation has led to a new wave of interest in using computer games in schools. It is believed that through playing certain types of computer games, learners can develop the following skills and behaviours:

- creative problem solving
- calculated risk taking
- persistence
- attention to detail
- effective collaboration

These are skills that are valued highly in our increasingly knowledge-based economy, and which *'ideally would be regularly demonstrated at school'* [22] but which are not easy to teach in a traditional school environment. Why is this the case? It is mainly a question of motivation.

Motivation

A recent study by the MacArthur Foundation's Digital Media and Learning Program [24] found that nearly one third of all 12 to 17 year olds played computer games every day, and that three fourths said they played at least once a week. Playing computer games is also no longer an activity that people give up when they get older – and the audience for computer games is getting older. According to recent figures by the Entertainment Software Association, *'the average game player is 34 years old and has been playing games for 12 years'.* [25]

If playing computer games is now an integral part of our learners' lives, then it makes sense to bring it into the classroom in some way, even if this means just talking about it together in the same way you might talk about TV programmes, what your learners have seen at the cinema or the sports and hobbies they are interested in. As all good teachers know from experience, it's about motivating learners by personalising the content of lessons and making what you do inside the classroom relevant to their lives outside of it.

Thanks to recent research studies, we know more about motivation than we used to – unfortunately, many adolescents in particular consider studying and schoolwork to be the least rewarding activities they do, and *'when in class or doing homework students ... generally feel sad, passive, constrained, bored, detached, and lonely'*. [26]

Schneider, Csikszentmihalyi and Knauth [27] also report a strong negative relationship between being in an academic class and feeling motivated, which they explain by the fact that these learners *'tend to find most academic classroom activities unenjoyable and uninteresting'*.

Partly, the problem is that *'in school environments most tasks are imposed on the students without involving them in designing their own learning schedules or choosing which activities to engage in'* [28]. Much of the time, extrinsic motivation (the need to pass exams, getting a better job, etc) is used by teachers to motivate learners but Daniel Pink, in his book *Drive* [29], illustrates why these extrinsic motivators are largely ineffective in today's society.

What are the problems with these 'carrot and stick' methods? They can extinguish any intrinsic motivation, diminish performance, crush creativity and foster short-term thinking, among other things. Pink suggests the three key elements of truly effective motivation are autonomy, mastery, and purpose.

Taking all this into account, we believe that the key motivating principles behind adding some kind of digital play content to your curriculum are these:

- The content that is most likely to motivate today's learners is probably already a part of their lives outside the classroom.
- Many classrooms have the technology to reach outside the classroom and can also reach the expectations that learners have of how they would like to see it used.

To motivate learners we have to engage them in our classrooms in a similar way to how they are engaged when playing a computer game.

● Engagement

In an age marked by ADHD (Attention Deficit Hyperactivity Disorder), and with more and more teachers complaining of the short attention spans of their learners, it can come as a surprise to observe the persistence, effort and concentration required to progress through the levels of an average console computer game.

What is clear here is that digital games are not only popular, but they are also often deeply engaging. What is it about them that makes them so? Would it be possible for educators to tap into this to make the content of the school curriculum more engaging?

A number of commentators have noticed this link between learning and games:

- *'Many parents and teachers complain about the short attention spans of their kids; but those same kids seem to have more than adequate attention spans when it comes to gaming.'* [31]
- *'Games are puzzles to solve, just like everything else we encounter in life. They are on the same order as learning to drive a car, or picking up the mandolin, or learning your multiplication tables ... the only real difference between games and reality is that the stakes are lower with games.'* [32]
- *'Fun from games arises out of mastery. It arises out of comprehension. It is the act of solving puzzles that makes games fun. In other words, with games, learning is the drug.'* [33]

What this information suggests is that learning is essentially fun if presented in the right way. In the classroom, you can try to recreate this sense of fun by adding elements of mystery and trying to turn dull exercises into stimulating puzzles. As we shall see, you can also use actual computer games with your learners in ways that are pedagogically valid, but sometimes it's enough just to recognise the interest they may have in computers and gaming.

As with anything that occupies so much of our free time, there's usually a need to explain why we are interested in it. Usually this will only happen, though, if we find an audience who shows an interest. Learners who play games love to talk about them. Knowing this is important, as it can be tapped into by teachers. Try talking about games and you may find that you've stumbled onto a 'hot topic' – one that your learners will talk about at length without much encouragement. All that is needed is for you to show an interest and be somewhat informed about the digital games they play, so you can talk the same language as your learners, and ask the right questions.

◯ Flow

So what do we teachers need to know about games? An important factor which sets computer games apart from other audiovisual media such as cinema and TV is the element of interactivity. It's usually the interactivity that counts in a game (often referred to as 'gameplay') – it's what makes the game exciting and what drives people to keep on playing. It comes from wanting to know what happens next, the sense of building your own narrative, of being inside a story.

Good gameplay is all about capturing the attention of a player and transporting them to a state where they are so engaged in playing they forget how long they have been playing for. This is also an optimal learning state which the psychologist Csikszentmihalyi has called 'flow' [35]. Athletes and gamers often refer to this as 'being in the zone' and it is the state of immersion and clarity you enter when you are experiencing absolute concentration on a task. It can happen in a classroom too.

When there's *flow* in a classroom activity, learners might lose track of time and nothing else seems to matter. When your learners tell you that something was 'fun' or ask 'Has the class finished already?' then they may have experienced flow. It's the opposite of having learners constantly looking at the time during class, waiting for it to end.

Flow usually happens when a person's mind or body is stretched to its limits in order to accomplish something that is both difficult, but not too difficult, and worthy of effort. A necessary condition for flow is that the goals of an activity need to be clear. It is also interesting to note that, in a game, flow is facilitated by immediate feedback although this interrupts flow in a class.

◯ Benefits

Game designers have also become much better at teaching players how to play their games. James Paul Gee, who is a professor of Literary Studies at Arizona State University, argues that there are 36 important learning principles which are inherently built into good computer games. These include skills such as *active and critical learning, a regime of competence* and *a commitment to learning*. Many of them can be applied to language learning, not least of which these three principles. In short, we want our learners to be active and critical in their language acquisition, to stick with it and also endeavour to improve.

And Gee is not alone. Marc Prensky, author of *Don't Bother Me Mom – I'm Learning* [37], similarly argues for the pedagogical benefits of computer games and shows how today they are training a younger generation in vital social skills. His book is aimed at parents and educators, proposing that many of the prejudices that we hold against computer games are in fact holding social development back.

Can computer games really be so beneficial? Toine Manders, a Dutch member of the European Parliament, thinks so and wrote in a report:

'Video games are in most cases not dangerous. We heard evidence from experts on computer games and psychologists from France (who) told us that video games have a positive contribution to make to the education of minors.' [38]

The Scottish government took this a step further in 2008 and ran trials in primary schools using computer game consoles to see if they boosted performance. Interestingly enough, the study [39] found that not only did it lead to higher attainment but also to better behaviour.

It should be clear by now that games are evolving into complex media and have a role to play in 21st century education. But what about in language learning?

Computer games and language learning

'Playing a game is not like watching one ninety-minute movie; it's like watching one whole season of a TV show – and watching it in a state of staring, jaw-clenched concentration.'
Nicholson Baker [40]

Computer games have come a long way in a short space of time. Some of the changes that are worth noting include the stunningly impressive graphics and the authentic sound effects which are often cited as being the hallmarks of a successful game. Another change that is not so obvious is the increasingly strong narrative element. Storytelling in games is becoming more sophisticated and realistic, and this aspect is ripe for exploitation in the language classroom. For this reason, you will find many activities in Part B of *Digital Play* that draw upon learners' existing knowledge of narrative gameplay, encouraging them to produce language.

Apart from being rich sources of narrative, many of these new games contain language (specifically English) that has to be understood and often used in order for players to fully participate in them. Depending on the game, this language can either be content to be understood (eg the audio may be in English, with subtitles in the player's language) or, more interestingly, if the gameplay takes place online, then it could involve real negotiated communication taking place between players.

⚪ Communication skills

'L2 education ... need(s) to examine (and create) gaming environments that are not only learning tools, but which also serve as critical contemporary arenas for task-relevant communication and relationship building.'
Ravi Purushotma, Steven Thorne and Julian Wheatley [41]

Whether it is a *MMORPG* (Massively Multiplayer Online Role-Playing Game) such as *World of Warcraft* or the richly absorbing experience of a modern console game, there is no doubt that online gaming is promoting international communication more than ever. Players use text chat and often headsets with microphones, speaking to other gamers to co-ordinate events in real time. With the proliferation of broadband internet, voice chat has become a more effective, convenient and fun way to communicate. It provides a much richer and co-operative gaming experience and, for the most part, these players will be communicating in English.

In these types of games, players organise themselves into groups (popularly called 'guilds' or 'clans') to socialise, co-ordinate team actions, discuss strategy, negotiate the trading of in-game objects, make announcements and generally report on events occurring within the game. Most of these games take place in real time and within what is called a 'persistent universe'. That is, the game persists – and doesn't stop – if you are not playing. For this reason, a lot of communication between players acts to keep people up-to-date on what they may have missed.

Communication between players also takes place outside of the game, too. On forums and websites, more people are sharing their interest in games and pooling their collective knowledge of tips and strategies.

There is so much potential here for language learning. In particular, we believe that this interest in computer games can be used to engage learners effectively when it comes to practising different skills – both communication skills in general and language skills in particular. The nature of some types of games means they have information gaps built into their design that can be easily exploited for live listening activities or writing practice, to stimulate speaking and encourage intensive reading.

Language skills

Computer games used to be all about reading. When home computing was in its infancy, the most popular type of game consisted of just a screen of text and a simple question waiting to be answered: What do you want to do next? *'As you typed in commands and sentences, the games would tell you a story; a story fraught with danger, excitement, puzzles and hours of exploration.'* [43]

These text adventures (also referred to as 'adventure games' and 'interactive fiction') would engage players, who would spend hours immersed in them, testing their thinking skills and using written language to solve puzzles and complete the adventures.

These games also depended on the players understanding an interesting range of vocabulary and being able to use the right verb and string sentences together to accomplish the task in hand. Because of this, there has recently been a resurgence of interest in using this type of interactive fiction (games such as *Zork* and *Colossal Cave*) for English language teaching and learning. [44]

As computers became more sophisticated, the graphics in games became much better. Text in *COTS* (Commercially Off The Shelf) games started to take a back seat and gameplay became less about understanding text and reading and writing instructions.

That does not mean, however, that reading does not play a part in contemporary *COTS* games. Written text still plays a large part in some. It is used in player instructions (either how to play the game or information about what to do in a quest) and is often displayed as character dialogue. Occasionally the written text is used as background to the story of the game, at other times understanding this written text is absolutely crucial to knowing what to do next: players are either skimming the text to get the gist of it, or looking for key words that tell them what action they need to perform.

Apart from written text, many *COTS* computer games offer opportunities for listening practice. Although some console games are now released with soundtracks recorded in different languages, many are still offered in English, with foreign language subtitles. The amount of spoken dialogue is not insubstantial. One typical example is *EverQuest II*, which contains some 59,233 lines of recorded dialogue (approximately 500 hours of speech). The purpose of much of this dialogue is to add atmosphere, and many games contain 'cut scenes' that fill in the story between game quests. There are also times, however, when understanding what a character says is crucial. Because of this, it is fair to say that a typical learner who plays computer games will receive a huge amount of English listening practice outside of the classroom.

Unlike *COTS* games, most popular online games do not have much spoken dialogue (if any), which is why the key to using them to practise language skills often lies in the design of the task that learners are asked to undertake. An alternative, of course, would be to use games already designed for language practice, but the majority of these games are flawed.

Language learning games

Although there are notable exceptions, most games specifically designed for language learning are not very good games. In theory, they should be ideal for learners, what with their graded language and being designed around specific lexical sets or grammar. In reality, the majority of the games available that have been specially written for language learning are less than compelling.

The tendency has so far been to simply take best practices from the classroom or self-access learning and try to replicate these on screen, adding an element of fun – and labelling the resulting activity as a computer game. Media scholar Henry Jenkins has noted that choosing a learning object and trying to fashion a gaming experience around it *'typically results in a game that combines the pedagogical value of a bad video game with the entertainment value of a bad textbook'*. [46]

> 'Although video games have not replaced reading ... they have changed the nature of reading and writing activities in which many young people engage.'
> James Paul Gee [42]

> 'We need to recognize that starting with the language learning objective, then subsequently designing a game around it, is not only doomed to produce a boring game, but will not even produce a pedagogically effective game.'
> Ravi Purushotma, Steven Thorne and Julian Wheatley [45]

In our experience, most language learning computer games end up being thinly disguised tests. They are usually overtly language-based and, typically, test knowledge of language through hand-to-eye co-ordinated or timed reflex games. Unfortunately, these games usually do not take into account some of the factors that make modern computer games so popular and such a commercial and cultural phenomenon. They often include unimpressive graphics, inauthentic sound effects and weak (or entirely missing) narrative elements. The end result usually draws a negative response from the learners that can have teachers scratching their heads and wondering why using these games does not work.

For these reasons, in *Digital Play* we have chosen to suggest existing online games that have not been specially designed for language learning. The games we use are first and foremost ones that have proven to be popular. We prefer to choose this type of game and build language skills practice and learning *within the tasks*. You could say that rather than 'language learning games', our approach is to use 'games in language learning'. The difference between these descriptions may seem slight, but they are actually (virtual) worlds apart.

Games in language learning

Communicative language learning is concerned with doing real things with language:

- Language education now prioritises negotiation of meaning and communicative use above structural language drills.
- Learners should be engaged in *using* the language, not talking *about* the language.

It follows that the best way for this to occur is when learning is embedded in communication.

Unfortunately, in many school contexts, communication is sidelined and the *understanding of the language* is often the main (sometimes only) goal in class. Knowing how to to talk about language is prioritised. In contrast, out of school, children *'generally understand and use languages as a means for communication, information gathering and gaming'*. [48]

This 'meaningful purpose' for using language with a *real audience* and, as Mark Warschauer says, *'to be able to use English to have a real impact on the world'* [49] is what gives most satisfaction when learning. What computer games can bring to language learning is that meaningful purpose, but it is usually only when a carefully designed task is introduced that language learning will be able to take place.

So, task design is the key, but what counts as a *task*?

In Task-Based Language Learning it is commonly agreed that a task is simply *'an activity or goal that is carried out using language'* [50]. Tasks that are designed to promote the use of computer games for language learning, however, need to be more than this. They need to be activities which promote the practice of language but which do not take the fun out of playing the game:

- What creates much of the fun when playing a computer game comes from the fact that people enjoy exercising control in difficult circumstances.
- What stops people from being able to exercise that control in many types of games is a lack of knowledge or information.

For this reason, this *information gap* is usually the starting point for any task.

As well as the importance of tasks, it is also necessary for feedback to occur, in order to draw the learner's attention away from the content and onto form. As Rod Ellis points out: *'Instruction needs to ensure that learners focus predominantly on meaning; secondarily, however, instruction should still include focus on form.'* [51]

When playing a game in class, you will have to decide how much time you dedicate to play (ie language practice) and how much to explicit language instruction (ie declarative knowledge about language). This will depend on the nature of the learning context and situation, and is an important decision that needs to be made by the person who is teaching.

'The growing use of games in learning may signal a new pedagogical approach to educating the millennial generation.'
Richard Van Eck [47]

Computer games and language teaching

We have seen how computer games can provide a context for language acquisition and so are well suited to the communicative goals of the foreign language classroom. Because games are all about the performance of skills within a system, players do *'not think about the language in use, but only about the action and where it might lead next'.* [53]

Teachers can use this to focus on language acquisition, often with surprising results. But simply playing a game with learners is never enough. The teacher must ensure that, each time a game is played, there is a context to allow language learning or practice to take place. We also recommend that a teacher does some groundwork before starting to introduce digital play to a class. For example, you may not normally play computer games in your own free time but, if you don't play yourself, you will be missing out on what your learners feel when *they* play.

A priori

The best way to begin is by putting your learners first. You will need to find out and understand what part games play in their lives. This can be done informally (simply ask them in class to tell you) or more formally (eg through the use of a survey – see the 'Game on' activities in Part B of this book for examples you can use).

You should also learn the language of games. This doesn't mean you have to start playing endless games yourself (although some experience of this will help you understand their appeal), but you do need to know enough to be able to ask the right questions. We hope that this book, of course, will give you enough information to be able to start talking to your learners knowledgeably about games!

We also recommend introducing games into your syllabus when it makes sense to do so. Rather than simply as an extra or a break from learning, teachers should decide to use a game to practise particular language because that is the particular language that is being studied or practised in class. Defining the learning goal when playing a game should be a given. This way, your learners will associate digital play with both the teaching and the learning in the classroom – and think of the whole experience in a positive way.

Another choice the teacher will have to make is what *type* of game to play. Browsing Part B of this book, you will see that we tend to use specific types of games because they lend themselves best to language teaching and learning. A discussion of appropriate game genres and the reasons for using them follows Part A of the book.

Many of the activities in *Digital Play* do not require access to computers and do not involve playing games during class time. Often, however, these activities will require you to do things in preparation – such as find images or look for information to bring into the classroom.

Planning a digital play activity well is also an important part of the process. Some of the activities we suggest may only involve you and your learners talking about games (this is still 'digital play', though) and many of them require very little time to set up. However, if playing a game *is* involved, it is always a good idea for you to spend some time playing it, to get a feel for how it would work in your own teaching context. You may also notice something that we have missed, or may come up with a better way of utilising the game with your learners.

A fortiori

Sometimes when it comes to teaching using games we are asked the question: Can computer games really help people learn a language? Given the hopefully convincing arguments we have been defending, this is in many ways the wrong question to ask. The question is: *How* do computer games help people learn a language? A game does not act alone. As we have seen, to be useful for language learning and practice, games need to have a context, which is usually provided by a task. The role of the teacher as facilitator is also crucial.

It is difficult to generalise, because each game is unique, but when games are used in teaching, the teacher's job is to react according to the situation. You need to give yourself to whatever the moment brings. You can vary the pace of an activity, let things go on longer than expected or bring them to a halt before you had planned. The important thing is to make sure the learning potential that exists in playing the game is realised. Learners should understand that there is a pedagogical reason for playing a game (it's not just to have some fun or take a break from studying), and this needs to be made clear.

Equally important is knowing when to interrupt the learners playing a game and how often you should do this. Too often, and you will kill the fun. Too little, and you will miss the learning opportunities. Facilitating in this way comes with practice, but here are a couple of tips that should help you:

- First of all, look out for any moments during gameplay when you think would be appropriate to interrupt the learners and focus on form or ask them to reflect on what they have been doing with language.
- The second tip draws on the world of cinema, where an oft-cited rule of storytelling is: 'Don't tell, show'. When it comes to games, the key is: 'Don't tell or show, play'. When using games for *teaching*, however, the most important part, the part where the learning occurs, will often only come if a teacher takes enough time to show or tell the learners. Frequently, this crucial part of the process will come *after* the game has been played.

A posteriori

As a general rule, after you have been playing a computer game with learners, it is a good idea to follow this up with some time set aside for reflection back in the classroom or in 'class formation' when the game playing has finished. If a game had a story you can ask the learners to retell it. If they were introduced to new vocabulary, then this can be reviewed or recorded in vocabulary notebooks.

Many computer games lend themselves well to being followed by writing tasks. The learners can be asked to predict what they think happens next after playing the beginning of a game. They can write character profiles or compose letters of advice to other players or to the game characters themselves. Then, of course, there are game reviews and comparisons of different games that can be set as post-playing tasks. These can be done in class or at home.

'Gamifying' homework is an option well worth pursuing. For instance, we have found that learners will voluntarily read more than they usually would. Give them a text that is linked to a game they have been playing, and necessary for that game to be completed, and the learners will happily read it at home, even if the text is a lot longer than those they usually read in English. In this way, a teacher can assign extensive reading that will often be gratefully received by learners as 'play' and not treated as 'homework'.

Computer games and language aims

While language learning and practice should be fun, engaging and motivational, it should also be relevant to the learners' current or future lives. Dörnyei [58] suggests that there are three primary motivational sources when it comes to learning another language. These are the learners' vision of themselves as effective speakers of the language, social pressure and positive learning experiences.

Many learners – teenagers in particular – will be more attuned to gaming than their teachers. That said, while they will be the experts in *play*, their teachers are the experts in *language*. It is particularly important to keep this in mind when you choose to do anything which is entertaining with your learners – and to remember not to let the activity itself distract from the language aims (ie the reason for doing it).

We have seen how the motivation to compete, and to complete digital play tasks, can potentially drive language acquisition – and this will work best if you integrate digital play into your syllabus rather than treat it as something special or divorced from what you usually do with your learners. If you start by finding out about their preferences and their playing habits early on, then it will be easier to do this – you can find activities to help you with this in the 'Game on' chapter of *Digital Play*.

Classes with elements of digital play should therefore be run in the same way you would manage any other class. The difference is that you will sometimes have to manage extra equipment, digital materials and different kinds of spaces.

⬤ Space

The teacher has a number of 'spaces' to think about when it comes to games. There is the all-important *game space*, which can provide a context for a number of activities, many of which are outlined in Part B of *Digital Play*.

The experience of playing games also increasingly relates to spaces outside of the game. There are now many *virtual spaces* on the internet where gamers talk about different games, share tips and advice, make friends and establish new social relationships based on gameplaying. As their teacher, you will want to investigate some of these spaces, especially as written English predominates, given that they can be a rich source of material for classroom discussion. It is also here that the teacher will be able to find solutions and clues to the completion of games that can form the raw material for language teaching tasks.

However, the *classroom space* is perhaps the most important one for teachers to consider. Although a lot of activities in this book have been designed to take place in any classroom, and require little or no technology, there are many others that are designed to take advantage of actually playing games with the learners. The way we envisage this happening means there are three different teaching scenarios where digital play can take place, and which reflect the chapters into which we have organised Part B:

- A simple 'non-connected' classroom space which does not have any technology.
- A classroom with a data projector, computer and broadband internet access, where there may also be an interactive whiteboard. We have called this the 'connected' classroom.
- A classroom with several computers with broadband internet connections – 'multiple' connections. Often these spaces are computer rooms or labs, where teachers can take learners from time to time. This space could also be the usual classroom, however, where there may be a set of laptops available.

For most language teachers, one of the important factors in the last two of these scenarios to consider will be how to manage the equipment.

⬤ Equipment

When playing games in a computer room or a classroom equipped with laptops, the key is to remember that the technology is there to help you teach and your learners practise or learn the language – this is the reason for using the equipment. Above all, you need to be careful not to fall into the trap of letting learners play computer games for their own sake.

If you have already looked at the games in Part B of this book, you might have noticed that not only have we chosen to focus upon games which are free, but also on those which are online and which can be played in any browser. There are good reasons for this. First, we appreciate that teachers or organisations will find it difficult or impossible to justify spending money on games. We also know from experience that, in many situations, teachers do not have permission to install software, which is why we have largely avoided choosing games which need to be downloaded.

Another choice we made concerns the platform. Although the most interesting games available at the moment have been made for gaming consoles such as Microsoft's Xbox 360,

'Digital games are, at their heart, problem-solving spaces that use continual learning and provide pathways to mastery through entertainment and pleasure.'
James Paul Gee [59]

'We cannot assume that just because children are growing up with these technologies that they use them or use them well, creatively and safely. The role of the teacher in guiding technology use is more important now than ever.'
Kathleen McGeady [60]

Sony's PlayStation 3 or Nintendo's Wii, there are few teachers who have this equipment available in the classroom or who will be able to persuade their school to buy one of them. The same is true of the portable gaming consoles (Nintendo's DS, Sony's PSP, etc).

Although there are schools now that are experimenting with class sets of handheld gaming consoles, this does not reflect the reality for most language teaching situations. That does not mean, however, that the activities in *Digital Play* cannot be adapted for console games if you find yourself in the (enviable) position of having access to one or more of these.

◯ Materials

One of the first decisions anyone who is looking to use games with language learners has to face is what games to use. There are so many different types of games out there now that this is not a question of being short of choice. However, when we started to investigate the use of games in the language learning classroom ourselves, some genres seemed obvious candidates: online games that include an information gap built into them (puzzle games, some adventure games, etc) were the best ones as far as language production is concerned.

Although we have said we are mainly concerned in this book with the sorts of computer games that can be found and played for free online, we will occasionally refer to games that need to be downloaded or that can be bought and played on a game console. It will be made clear when this is the case. You will also see that we concentrate on types of digital games in which the player takes on the role of a character, and/or that require the solving of various problems. There are, of course, lots of other digital games, but we have found that these puzzle games are those that can be best adapted to language classroom use.

On the following pages, you will find a selection of online games that can be used to practise skills work with learners. Then in Part B, you will find activities that deal with these types, and others.

In short, our experience has shown that today's learners respond well to the use of computer games for language learning and, if appropriate tasks are provided, the result can not only be a very motivating but also a stimulating educational experience. The beliefs and practices embodied in *Digital Play* offer the ways and means to be able to introduce computer games into your syllabus and provide you with a large number of different ideas on how to do this.

We are in the midst of a digital revolution that affects us all and which should not (and cannot) be ignored by the world of education. By bringing a little of this digital revolution to the classroom, we will help our learners be better prepared for the 21st century, but we need to do so by integrating digital play into what we do, without forgetting that we are language teachers and that our language aims for our learners must be the *raison d'être* of our pedagogy.

The authors hope that this book will inspire you to bring elements of the digital revolution taking place outside the classroom – inside. But before setting out in Part B the 'game plans' that make up the core element of *Digital Play*, we thought to incorporate the following brief reference sections that readers – especially, but not exclusively, those teachers starting off on the road to digital play – may find useful:

'Students are not just using technology differently today, but are approaching their life and their daily activities differently because of the technology.'
Net Day [61]

'When learning stops, fun stops, and playing eventually stops. For humans, real learning is always associated with pleasure and is ultimately a form of play.'
James Paul Gee [62]

Bibliography

1. Aldrich, C *Learning Online with Games, Simulations and Virtual Worlds* Jossey-Bass 2009
2. Klopfer, E, Osterweil, S and Salen, K 'Moving Learning Games Forward' (white paper) *Education Arcade* 2009 http://www.educationarcade.org/
3. Crawford, C *The Art of Computer Game Design* McGraw Hill 1984
4. Marc Prensky during his plenary speech at 43rd Annual IATEFL Conference, Cardiff, UK 2009
5. Gee, J P *What Video Games Have to Teach Us about Learning and Literature* Palgrave MacMillan 2003
6. Shaffer, D W *How Computer Games Help Children Learn* Palgrave MacMillan 2006
7. Koster, R *A Theory of Fun for Game Design* Paraglyph Press 2005
8. Poole, S *Trigger Happy: The inner life of video games* Fourth Estate 2000
9. Kutner, L and Olson, C K *Grand Theft Childhood: The Surprising Truth about Violent Video Games* Simon & Schuster 2008
10. Kahne, J, Middaugh, E and Evans, C 'The Civic Potential of Video Games' The John D and Catherine T MacArthur Foundation Reports on Digital Media and Learning 2009 http://mitpress.mit.edu/books/full_pdfs/Civic_Potential_of_Games.pdf
11. Chatfield, T *Fun Inc: Why games are the 21st century's most serious business* Virgin Books 2010
12. Carr, D 'Games and Gender' In Carr, D, Buckingham, D, Burn, A and Schott, G *Computer Games: Text, Narrative and Play* Polity 2001
13. Krotoski, A *Chicks and Joysticks: An Exploration of Women and Gaming* Entertainment and Leisure Software Publishers Association 2004
14. Casas, F 'Video Games: Between Parents and Children' In Hutchby, I and Moran-Ellis, J (Eds) *Children, Technology and Culture* Falmer 2001
15. Schott, G and Kambouri, M 'Social Play and Learning' In Carr, D, Buckingham, D, Burn, A and Schott, G *Computer Games: Text, Narrative and Play* Polity 2001
16. Gee, J P op. cit.
17. Prensky, M *Don't Bother Me Mom – I'm Learning* Paragon House 2006
18. Prensky, M 'Digital Natives, Digital Immigrants' 2001 http://www.marcprensky.com/writing/
19. Palfrey, J and Gasser, U *Born Digital: Understanding the First Generation of Digital Natives* Basic Books 2008
20. Chatfield, T op. cit.
21. Gee, J P op. cit.
22. Klopfer, E, Osterweil, S and Salen, K op. cit.
23. Armando Baltra, Professor in the Department of Early Childhood Education, California State University, USA
24. Kahne, J, Middaugh, E and Evans, C op. cit.
25. Entertainment Software Association 'Industry Facts' 2010 http://www.theesa.com/facts/index.asp
26. Wong, M M and Csikszentmihalyi, M 'Motivation and academic achievement: The effects of personality traits and the quality of experience' *Journal of Personality 59*, 1991
27. Schneider, B, Csikszentmihalyi, M and Knauth, S 'Academic challenge, motivation and self-esteem: The daily experiences of students in high school' In Hallinan, M T (Ed) *Restructuring schools: Promising practices and policies* Plenum Press 1995
28. Dörnyei, Z 'Motivation and motivating in the foreign language classroom' *Modern Language Journal 78*, 1994
29. Pink, D *Drive: The surprising truth about what motivates us* Riverhead Books 2010
30. Norman, D quoted in Prensky, M *Don't Bother Me Mom – I'm Learning* Paragon House 2006
31. Palfrey, J and Gasser, U op. cit.
32. Koster, R op. cit.
33. Koster, R op. cit.
34. Jenkins, H *The Wow Climax: Tracing the Emotional Impact of Popular Culture* New York University Press 2007
35. Csikszentmihalyi, M *Flow* Random House 1992
36. Gee, J P 'Video Games, New Teaching Tool' *Channel 3000* 2005 http://www.channel3000.com/education/4121724/detail.html
37. Prensky, M *Don't Bother Me Mom – I'm Learning* Paragon House 2006
38. Manders, T quoted in 'Video games are good for children: EU report' *The Guardian* 2009 http://www.guardian.co.uk/technology/2009/feb/12/computer-games-eu-study
39. Miller, D J and Robertson, D P 'Educational benefits of using game consoles in a primary classroom: A randomised controlled trial' *British Journal of Educational Technology* 2010 http://onlinelibrary.wiley.com/doi/10.1111/j.1467-8535.2010.01114.x/full
40. Baker, N 'Painkiller Deathstreak: Adventures in video games' *The New Yorker* 2010 http://www.newyorker.com/reporting/2010/08/09/100809fa_fact_baker
41. Purushotma, R, Thorne, S L and Wheatley, J '10 Key Principles for Designing Video Games for Foreign Language Learning' 2009 http://knol.google.com/k/10-key-principles-for-designing-video-games-for-foreign-language-learning
42. Gee, J P Foreword to Hutchinson, D *Playing to Learn: Video Games in the Classroom* The Book Depository 2007
43. Scott, J 'Get Lamp: A documentary film about adventures in text' 2009 http://www.getlamp.com/
44. Pereira, J 'Adventure Games and Interactive Fiction' Presentation given at IATEFL Annual Conference, Cardiff, UK 2009 http://www.theswanstation.com/IATEFL_09_files/IATEFL%20adventure%20games.pdf
45. Purushotma, R, Thorne, S L and Wheatley, J op. cit.
46. Jenkins, H *Convergence culture: Where old and new media collide* New York University Press 2006
47. Van Eck, R 'The digital natives are restless: Digital game-based learning and the future of education' *Educause Review 41(2)* 2006
48. Sørensen, B H and Meyer, B 'Serious games in language learning and teaching: A theoretical perspective' In 'Situated Play: Proceedings of DiGRA 2007 Conference' Digital Games Research Association 2007 http://www.digra.org/dl/db/ 07312.23426.pdf
49. Warschauer, M 'Technological change and the future of CALL' In Fotos, S and Browne, C M (Eds) *New Perspectives on CALL for Second Language Classrooms* Lawrence Erlbaum Associates 2004
50. Richards, J C and Rodgers, T S *Approaches and Methods in Language Teaching* Cambridge University Press 2001
51. Ellis, R 'Principles of Instructed Language Learning' *Asian EFL Journal* 2005 http://www.asian-efl-journal.com/May_2005_Conference_Ellis.php
52. Purushotma, R, Thorne, S L and Wheatley, J op. cit.
53. Kossuth, K C 'Artificial Intelligence and CALL' In Underwood, J H *Modern Media in Foreign Language Education: Theory and Implementation* National Textbook Company 1987
54. Johnson, S *Everything Bad is Good for You* Penguin 2006
55. Linda Snow, Head of Oakdale School, Essex, UK, quoted in Chatfield, T *Fun Inc: Why games are the 21st century's most serious business* Virgin Books 2010
56. Burn, A quoted in Carr, D, Buckingham, D, Burn, A and Schott, G *Computer Games: Text, Narrative and Play* Polity 2001
57. Littlewood, W *Communicative Language Teaching: An introduction* Cambridge University Press 1981
58. Dörnyei, Z 'New ways of motivating foreign language learners: Generating vision' *Links 38*, Winter 2008
59. Gee, J P 'Deep Learning Properties of Good Digital Games: How Far Can They Go?' 2010 http://www.jamespaulgee.com/node/37
60. McGeady, K quoted in Topfield, J 'Digital Natives Restless' *The Age* 2010 http://www.theage.com.au/national/education/digital-natives-restless-20100820-1390k.html
61. 'The Speak Up National Research Project Summary' http://www.tomorrow.org/speakup/
62. Gee, J P *Situated Language and Learning: A critique of traditional schooling* Routledge 2004

A gaming glossary

A guide to digital play

Digital Play is full of special terms related to the world of computer games (the ubiquitous walkthrough, for example). We are sure that you will be familiar with many of these, but some will be new to you. For this reason, we present here a glossary we hope you will find useful.

As computer games have evolved, the medium has developed numerous distinctive genres, many of which can easily be adapted for the language classroom although not all are immediately appropriate for language learning. We begin by providing a list of game genres, including the following:

- a brief explanation describing the genre
- some links to specific examples
- a note on what we consider their relative strengths in relation to language teaching

In our opinion, it is worthwhile spending time getting acquainted with the types of games that work well with language learners.

Digital Play mainly concentrates on games that are free and can be found and played online or downloaded to your computer. But be warned: some of the examples in the 'Great games' section may be only available as commercial console games. We included these, as they are very well known. There are also a few activities in Part B that call for discussion, reading reviews, writing from screenshots, or watching trailers that these examples are intended for.

Game genres

◯ Action

Action games are characterised by emulating challenges that, in the real world, are reliant on physical strength, endurance and reaction speed. You guide your game character through a hostile world, collecting objects, avoiding obstacles and defeating enemies with various weapons and attack moves. This genre has proved to be the most commercially successful, with games selling in their millions.

Action games	compactiongames.about.com
Computer action games	computeractiongames.org

Strong storylines, along with engaging and colourful characters, make these games great for stimulating written work. Creative story writing, describing physical appearance and personality traits and narrating 'live' newscasts are just a few examples demonstrated in Part B of *Digital Play*.

◯ Adventure

Adventure games place importance on storyline and a strong narrative. An adventure game usually involves a central character that explores the game world, solves puzzles and finally reaches the end of the game which offers a conclusion to the story. The stories themselves can be fictional or based on true events.

Adventure computer games	adventurecomputergames.net
Adventure games	adventurecomputergames.org

As well as having interesting stories, these games often have audio or written texts to support the gaming experience which, in turn, provide a great opportunity for receptive skills work in either listening or reading and, at times, a combination of the two.

Arcade

Arcade games generally rely on reaction speeds and hand–eye coordination. Passing from one stage to another usually means completing a simple task within a short, specific time limit. The next stage and subsequent levels usually require the player to complete the same task but with an increasing complexity or in a faster time. Why not play a few of these games and judge for yourself if your learners would like them?

Arcade games	www.arcadegames.org
Free classic arcade games	www.freeclassicgames.com

These games are excellent for the choral drilling of directions in a connected classroom with you on the keyboard and your learners shouting out the instructions. You can also offer limited game playing time on these games as an incentive or reward for doing language work from, say, a coursebook.

Casual

Many of the different game types listed in this glossary can also fall into the category of 'casual games', as long as the game itself requires little in the way of skill or that the gamer plays continuously. Usually, short bursts of game playing and mass audience appeal are typical attributes of a casual game.

Casual game association	www.casualgamesassociation.org
Free casual games	free-casual-game.com

Casual games are great resources for extracting and listing the vocabulary and discrete language items that arise during play. After play, a look at building word groups, focusing on word stress and practising pronunciation can all be useful language activities.

Dressing up

Dressing up games are digital versions of scrapbook cut-and-paste paper dolls, only the variety can range from period costume to 21st century fashion, through to superheroes and on to monsters. The games are characterised by an *avatar* (fictional or real, creatures or people) that acts as a template upon which the player can choose, place and colour clothes, accessories and physical features.

Dress up games	www.dressupgames.com
Click dress up games	www.clickdressupgames.com

Dressing up games lend themselves well to skills work dealing with the vocabulary of clothes and parts of the body. There are also other ways of using these games for language use which you will find in Part B of the book. For instance, many online dressing up sites now allow you to make friends and chat with other players, as well as sharing and displaying your dressed up characters.

Escape the room

Escape the room games usually take place within a single room or a building with a number of accessible rooms. The gameplay usually begins with you finding that you have been locked in a room and have to find your way out. You explore the rooms by 'pointing and clicking' on various objects in order to find hidden objects. These hidden objects can then be used or combined with other objects in order to solve puzzles that will finally allow you to escape.

Escape the room games	www.escapetheroomgames.net
Escape games	www.escapegames24.com

A teacher armed with the solution in the form of a guide (*walkthrough*) can help learners to escape from the room by giving them clues in either written or oral form. The beauty of this type of information gap activity is that it works well for practising different skills. You can also get learners working together in pairs to discuss how to solve the game.

◉ First person shooter (FPS)

In a 'shoot 'em up' style combat game, you view and experience the action from the perspective of the game character. The gameplay involves killing numerous enemies, using weapon-based combat while exploring the game world and completing missions. This genre has produced some of the most critically acclaimed and commercially successful video games.

First person shooter games   first-person-shooter.freeonlinegames.name
FPS games   first-person-shooter.games14.net

Due to the notoriety of these games, they can provide a convenient platform on which to discuss a number of topics. Discussing storylines, narrating cut scenes from the game, listening to trailers, reading game strategies and reviews, as well as discussing the controversial aspects of video games, can all be engaging activities.

◉ Hidden objects

A hidden objects game typically challenges the player to find items on a list that are hidden within a picture (of a cluttered room, for instance), usually within a specified time limit. If a level is completed the player moves to a more difficult picture, has to find more items and has less time to find them – or a combination of these three challenges.

Play hidden object games   www.playhiddenobjectgames.net
Object hidden games   objecthiddengames.com

These games can be effective for vocabulary development when used as an open-class activity in a connected classroom. Learners writing down or shouting out items and their location is fun way to have some friendly competition while learning.

◉ Incentive

These are games that provide an incentive to work, offering rewards for tasks and chores that would otherwise be routine, in order to make them more fun. There is currently a lot of interest in this potential of 'gamifying' work. Here are two examples:

Chore Wars   www.chorewars.com
Epic Win   www.rexbox.co.uk/epicwin

You can use these games to provide learners with a 'fun' reward after having completed a controlled language task, such as a test or an exercise from a coursebook that individuals or learners in general may be reluctant to complete or find boring to do. The games can also be used to record and present language learners' progress.

◉ Interactive fiction

Similar to a *Text adventure*, but with the story being supplemented by images or animation that is not just decorative, though the emphasis is still on reading.

Interactive fiction archive   www.ifarchive.org
Zarf's interactive fiction   eblong.com/zarf/if.html

Because of the amount of text that needs to be read to understand what to do next, these games can be great sources of interesting language for the classroom.

◉ Mobile

A game that has been developed to be downloaded, installed and played on a touch-screen-based smartphone or similar handheld device.

Android games   market.android.com/apps
Apple games   www.apple.com/iphone/apps-for-everything/fun-and-games.html

With so many people now playing games on mobile devices, it seems a shame not to take advantage. Ask your learners about the mobile games they play, get them to talk to each other about their favourites or show their partner one and explain how it works.

⬤ Platform

These are video games where the player has to use gaming skills to jump to and from platforms and navigates obstacles in order to achieve an objective and progress to the next level. Each subsequent level increases in difficulty.

Daily games   www.dailygames.com/platformgames.html
Game garage   www.gamegarage.co.uk/platform-games

Class activities that can be used with platform games include predicting what happens next and describing the obstacles that lie in the way of reaching the objective.

⬤ Point and click

This is a very sweeping term used to describe video games which involve moving the mouse cursor to certain areas on the screen (the 'point' part) and pressing one or more of the mouse buttons (the 'click' part).

Point and click games   www.pointnclickgames.com
Omigame   www.omigame.com/en/point-a-click.html

For some suggestions on how to use these games with learners, have a look at the *Adventure* and *Escape the room* sections here.

⬤ Puzzle

Puzzle games tend to be quite abstract and typically involve arranging geometric forms to progress through the levels (eg *Tetris*). The puzzles usually involve solving quite simple problems that test a player's awareness of patterns and/or short-term memory. Reaction speeds are not usually put to the test but, rather, the emphasis is more on finding a solution to a problem. Here are a few to challenge your puzzle-solving abilities:

Puzzle game yard   gameyard.com/puzzle
Puzzle factory   www.puzzlefactory.com

At times, these games have repetitive language elements that can be exploited in a similar way to *Arcade* games, but they can also be extended and expanded upon if learners are encouraged to produce instructions (written or spoken) while the game is paused.

⬤ Quiz

Often versions of TV quiz programmes, these are games in which individual players or teams attempt to answer questions correctly in order to score points and beat other players or teams. Questions can be based on a range of subjects from general knowledge to more specialised subjects.

Quiz 'em all   quiz-em-all.com
Squigly quizzes   squiglysplayhouse.com

Many of the more popular games can be downloaded in a template form and customised to target topics that your learners are interested in or target language you have covered in class. Examples of downloadable quizzes are included in the 'Some great games' section.

⬤ RPG

In roleplaying games you immerse yourself in the reality of the game world in which you are playing. This means staying in character when you communicate with other players by speaking (through a microphone) or, more commonly, by chatting (typing on a keyboard). RPGs have become part of popular culture in the form of the Massively Multiplayer Online Role-Playing Game (MMORPG). In these, numerous players interact together in real time and within a persistent world – offering anything from a confrontation with a dragon or a fight with fantastical creatures to an epic adventure in a world of elves and fairies.

EA RPG   www.ea.com/genre/rpg-games
RPGamer   www.rpgamer.com

Most language production in these games comes from a real need to communicate with other players, often in real time and during gameplay. There is also a lot of reading practice available, in the form of help forums that discuss game issues, share tips, strategies – and just general chat.

Simulation

Many of the available popular simulation games are based on real-life situations and, recently, many charitable organisations have commissioned simulation games to raise awareness of a particular social issue. There are games that focus on building an infrastructure to deal with natural disasters or examine the plight of the third world. Other simulation games involve players running a business or shop, or managing a real-world based organisation or football club, etc.

EA simulation games   www.ea.com/news/tag/simulation
Learn 4 good simulation   www.learn4good.com/games/simulation.htm

Life simulation games are perfect for discussing daily routines and the vocabulary of everyday objects in the home (rooms, furniture, etc). Strategy games can be used as a discussion platform for how natural disasters affect lives and what can be done to reduce their impact. Discussion games may invite learners to debate and vote on what course of action a third world farmer should take running a farm.

Singing and music

A competitive music or singing game is one in which players interact with a musical score or the lyrics of a song in order to complete puzzles that revolve around rhythm. It also involves some form of visual feedback to lead players through the game.

Karaoke games   karaoke.nettop20.com
Music games   www.musicgames.net

These games can provide a fun interlude in class, as well as providing a context for looking at music-based vocabulary or a focus on the language contained within the lyrics of a song.

Sports

These emphasise the playing of traditional physical sports events which the player emulates by using a computer interface device (such as the mouse or keyboard). Modern video game consoles now have controllers (eg the Microsoft Xbox 360 Kinect, the Nintendo Wii or the Sony PlayStation 3 Move) which allow for a more 'authentic' gameplay.

EA sports games   www.easports.com
Gamespot sports games   www.gamespot.com/sports

Providing a sports commentary, shouting crowd encouragement, discussing strategies and writing a report of a sports game event are just a few of the possible language tasks open to this type of game.

Text adventure

Very similar to *Interactive fiction*, these types of games were among some of the earliest computer games and you can still find many of them online. They are usually text-only: if graphics are present, they tend to be decorative in purpose or designed to support the written story much as illustrations in books do.

Choice of games   www.choiceofgames.com
If comp   www.ifcomp.org

Because of the language content, these games are usually only appropriate for reading and writing activities with advanced learners. After reading the text, the player has to decide what to do next. This involves typing in basic instructions such as *walk east*, *get lamp*, etc, and then reading how the game story develops as a result of these actions.

Virtual pet social sims

This is a specific type of simulation game that usually involves designing, creating and then looking after a single creature or creatures (real or fictional) within an environment that can be personalised by their owner – the game player. Many of these games revolve around a connected online community, much in the same way as described in the *Dressing up* games section. They are ideal for those who like little creatures, cute penguins or a large choice of different virtual pets.

Adopt Me   www.adoptme.com
Virtual pups   virtualpups.com

These games are very popular with young learners, and can be a fun way to introduce animal vocabulary, physical descriptions, abilities and colours. They can also be exploited for skills work, with descriptive writing and describing daily routines. With a little scaffolding, some grammatical complexity can be achieved with simple verb forms such as *to be*, *have got*, *can*, *is wearing*, etc.

Game guides

With the growth of gaming, a whole sub-genre of writing has exploded onto the scene. In forums, fans write opinions of a game's good and bad points. They may even be inspired to write their own fan fiction, adding depth and detail to game lore. Indeed, some of the most popular computer games have websites which include fan contributions, including tips and strategy guides.

These strategy guides sit side-by-side with FAQs (frequently asked questions) and both are usually found on websites connected directly with a specific game. There are also more detailed game instructions which help gamers complete a game right from the beginning through to the closing sequence. This is usually referred to as a 'walkthrough', although outside of gaming this term is not very well known.

The walkthrough

Because of the challenging nature of modern games, it is a given that a certain amount of frustration comes with the territory. There may be hidden bonuses or rewards, puzzles that are difficult to solve and challenges that at times seem almost impossible to overcome.

To help others, expert gamers will finish a game and then write instructions on how to find the bonuses and solve the puzzles, and give advice on how best to play. In turn, other gamers usually refer to these walkthroughs with a degree of respect and are careful not to cheat, but only read and use the sections that they need to.

In truth, there is a great demand for walkthroughs because many games are extremely difficult to finish without one. Steven Johnson, in his book *Everything Bad is Good for You*, talks about a little-known and appreciated facet of video games, saying that:

'the dirty little secret of gaming is how much time you spend not having fun. You may be frustrated; you may be confused or disoriented; you may be stuck'.

It is for this reason that game guides are so popular. The guidebook for the game *Grand Theft Auto*, for example, has sold more than 1.6 million copies. These guides usually include walkthroughs, the detailed step-by-step instructions of how to complete the game. For most games, walkthroughs are now available online. The easiest way for us to find one is to use an online search engine and write the 'name of the game' and then add a plus sign and the word 'walkthrough'.

Used while playing, a walkthrough scaffolds a language learner's gameplay. Gamers write and post these instructions not only to help fellow gamers complete a game but also to gain *kudos* as game experts. In their entirety, these instructions can be a simple list of half a dozen words (typical for simple online games) or far more complex, consisting of a text with a word count of around 16,000 words.

Of course, in language learning a walkthrough has too much potential content not to exploit it more fully. For teachers, it offers raw material that can be used to design tasks for the language classroom.

Because games with walkthroughs have information gaps built into them, teachers can easily create an activity exploiting this. It's best to start with the text and adapt it. Here are just a few ideas:

- **Gap fill**
  Blank out target language for learners to guess while playing. Removing verbs or nouns works equally as well as removing articles or adjectives.

- **Jigsaw reading**
  Learners order a cut-up walkthrough as they play the game.

- **Live listening**
  Read out the game instructions as a dictation, grading the language at a level appropriate for your learners.

- **Reading comprehension**
  Learners read the walkthrough and play the game, which becomes a comprehension check.

- **Target language areas**
  Rewrite a walkthrough to contain target grammar or vocabulary. This works very well with conditionals, sequencers, present tenses, verbs + prepositions (to express movement), phrasal verbs, etc.

It is perhaps worth remembering that it is also true that if there *is* a walkthrough to a game, then it is usually a good game.

Game sites

There are a number of websites you can go to, to find out more information about games. Here is just a small selection that we recommend you have a look at:

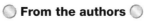 **From the authors**

Digital Play – digitalplay.info/blog
The blog that supports this book. We frequently publish ideas on how to use digital play, where to look online for resources and lesson plans for specific games.

Kyle's wiki – kylemawer.wikispaces.com
A wikispace by Kyle that indexes games by name and provides links to play the game, read the walkthrough and watch the video walkthrough.

Graham's blog – blog-efl.blogspot.com
Blog-EFL contains reflections on teaching and learning languages with ICT, including games and using virtual worlds.

 **From A–Z**

Armor Games – armorgames.com
The official site for a gaming company which produces a lot of very popular, visually engaging and challenging online games.

Big Blue Cup – www.bigbluecup.com/games.php
Home to an adventure game studio that helps you create your own 'point and click' adventure games as well as view some that others have made.

Bubblebox – www.bubblebox.com

A game website that stores lots of popular games all in one place so you needn't spend time surfing to find those online games to use in class.

Casual Girl Gamer – www.casualgirlgamer.com

A blog which lists games in categories (such as 'ten best games that use audio') and provides a short description and personal review of each one as well as a link to the game itself.

Cnet Games – www.cnet.com/games

Reviews and PC games to download.

Downloadable Games – downloads.games.co.uk/moreGames.aspx

An extensive range of downloadable games for you to adapt and use in class.

English Attack – www.english-attack.com

An innovative community website that uses clips from movies, TV series and online games, connecting learners to create a different way of improving language skills.

Flash Game – www.flash-game.net

A website specialising in free online Flash games.

Free Games – www.freeonlinegames.com

A website with a compilation of free online games, ordered by game genre.

Gamasutra – www.gamasutra.com

An online magazine for game developers that includes news, reviews and job posts.

Gamershood – www.gamershood.com

A game website with an extensive archive of online games conveniently classified into different game genres, awarded a star rating and accompanied with a link to walkthroughs.

Gametop – www.gametop.com

A site with a large selection of free PC games for downloading.

Guardian Games Blog – www.guardian.co.uk/technology/gamesblog

A great source for news, reviews and articles about the world of computer games.

Handheld Games Museum – www.handheldmuseum.com

A fascinating repository of information about handheld game machines as well as sections on video games in movies, game manuals, etc.

Inanimate Alice – www.inanimatealice.com

A series of interactive fiction stories that revolve around various events during the life of the central character: Alice.

Jay is Games – jayisgames.com

A website full of reviews and discussions of online and casual games, which includes walkthroughs to many of the games mentioned.

Joystiq – www.joystiq.com

The definitive source for news and information on the video game industry.

Kids Know It All – www.kidsknowit.com

A collection of educational games and activities for kids for different school subjects.

Larry Ferlazzo – larryferlazzo.edublogs.org

A prolific blogger with a plethora of online resources for language teachers to use with their classes (including games) or to assist with professional development.

Lingual Gamers – lingualgamers.com

An online thesis exploring language learning with new media and video games.

MMORPGS – www.mmorpg.com

Forums, news, games, reviews, blogs and photos of games covering this very popular genre of video games.

NASAGA – www.nasaga.org
A professional community of practice dedicated to the using of games and simulations to improve learning results.

Online Games – www.onlinegames.net
A search engine and website to help you find games, view ratings and play.

Pencil Kids – www.pencilkids.com
A limited selection, but more than compensated for by some very bright, fun and easily adaptable games.

Point 'n Click – www.pointnclickgames.com
A website that has a nice range of games covering this very broad and popular genre.

Popcap – www.popcap.com
Arcade and casual games that you can play online or download.

Quaser Games – www.quasargames.com
A large selection of free-to-play online games.

RPGs – www.freeonlinerpgs.org
A roleplaying games community where you can read, play and chat all about them.

Spawnpoint – www.spawnpoint.com
An online gaming portal and community.

Sploder – www.sploder.com/free-game-creator.php
A website that can help you make simple games. Great for project work.

Text Adventures – www.textadventures.co.uk
Reading skills work is only a few clicks away on this website that focuses on text-based adventure games.

U Got Games – www.ugotgames.com
A great place to go for that free Flash game that you want to use as a reward in class.

Ultimate Arcade – www.ultimatearcade.com
An online gaming company website offering downloadable games as well as ready-to-play online ones.

Virtual Pets – www.virtualpet.com/vp/links/links.htm
A website with a huge archive of virtual pet games, either ready to play online or to download.

World of Warcraft – battle.net/wow
The world's most popular fantasy roleplaying game that takes place in a virtual world inhabited by orcs, elves and humans.

X Gen Studios – www.xgenstudios.com
Home to a games company that designs, develops and publishes video games and hosts a popular games forum.

Yahoo Games – games.yahoo.com
Games for you to play online, download or purchase, covering a wide range of genres.

Zap Dramatic – www.zapdramatic.com
A game company whose gaming mission is to entertain and educate through serious games and dramatic simulations.

Some great games

Great to play, great to use

The 'Game genres' section explained the different types of video games and gave two example links. There's no reason why you can't use any of these with activities in Part B, as well as the games we have selected specifically for a particular activity.

Of course, once a game has been played and has been exploited to the full it is 'Game over'. We have therefore compiled a more comprehensive list of 'great games' for your language aims.

These commercially popular games can be:

- (–) played directly online: connected to the internet
- (d) played offline: downloaded and installed on a computer
- (c) played on a video game console: bought from a gaming shop
- (m) played on a mobile: usually a smartphone

This is our list:

Action
Back to the Future (d)
www.telltalegames.com/bttf
Battlestar Galactica
en.battlestar-galactica.bigpoint.com
Game Top (d)
www.gametop.com/category/
action.html
HALO (c)
www.halo.xbox.com/en-us/intel/
titles/haloreach
Jurassic Park (d)
www.telltalegames.com/jurassicpark
Monkey Island (d)
www.telltalegames.com/
monkeyisland
Tyrannosaurus Run
www.shockwave.com/gamelanding/
tyrannosaurus-run.jsp

Adventure
Adventure Games (d)
www.bestshareware.net/
adventure.htm
Anika's Odyssey
gambolio.com/#/game-play:16058
Arcane Season
www.gamershood.com/
flashgames/137

Featherweight (d)
www.bigbluecup.com/games.
php?action=detail&id=1231
Hetherdale
www.bubblebox.com/play/
adventure/1747.htm
Hotel (d)
games.softpedia.com/get/
Shareware-Games/Hotel.shtml
Prince of Persia (c)
www.prince-of-persia.com
Samorost 2
amanita-design.net/samorost-2
Shockwave (d)
www.shockwave.com/download/
adventure-games.jsp
Sam and Max (d)
www.telltalegames.com/
samandmax
Stage 07
www.stage07.com
Tomb Raider (c)
www.tombraider.com
Uncharted (c)
www.unchartedthegame.com

Animated film
123 Cartoon (d)
www.cutoutpro.com
D-Film
www.dfilm.com
Go Animate
goanimate.com
Xtra Normal
www.xtranormal.com
Zimmer Twins
www.zimmertwins.com

Arcade
Classic Arcade Games
www.classicgamesarcade.com
Pacman
www.freepacman.org
Pong
www.xnet.se/javaTest/jPong/
jPong.html
Rocket Escape
www.dailyfreegames.com/
flash/arcade-games/
rocket-escape.html
Space Invaders
www.freespaceinvaders.org
Sveerz (d)
www.miniclip.com/games/sveerz

Type 'em Up
flashgamesite.com/full/
915-TypeemUp
Word Attack
www.fupa.com/game/Word-flash-
games/word-attack.html

Casual
Bookworm (d)
www.popcap.com/games/free/
bookworm
Bowman
www.stickpage.com/
bowmangameplay.shtml
Farmville
www.farmville.com
Flow
interactive.usc.edu/projects/
cloud/flowing
Free Casual Game (d)
free-casual-game.com
Free Rice
www.freerice.com
Grammar Ninja
www.kwarp.com/portfolio/
grammarninja.html
Let's Get Bakin'
www.shockwave.com/
gamelanding/lets-get-bakin.jsp
Mafia Wars
http://www.mafiawars,com
Shopping Cart Hero
www.minijuegos.com/Shopping-
Cart-Hero/7668
Skyscraper Parcours
www.juegos247.net/juegos/
Skyscraper_Parcours
Solip Skier
mikengreg.com/solipskier

Dressing up
Fashion Games
www.fashiongames247.com/
online47-Dress-up-Games
Hero Machine
www.ugo.com/games/superhero-
generator-heromachine-2-5
High School Style Shop
girls-dressup.dressup.me/high-
school-style-shop.html
Marvel Heroes
marvel.com/games/play/31/
create_your_own_superhero

Pokemon Trainer
www.girlgames4u.com/pokemon-trainer-dress-up-game.html
Rainbow (d)
www.rainbowdressup.com/download-dressup-games.php
Rock Band
www.trendydressup.com/playgame/1215/rock-band.html

Escape the room
Arcade Cabin (d)
www.arcadecabin.com/page-downloadgames.html
Blue Chamber
www.fasco-csc.com/works/bluechamber/index_e.php
Classroom Escape
www.myescapegames.com/clasroom-escape.php
Crimson Room
www.fasco-csc.com/works/crimson/crimson_e.php
Escape the Kitchen
www.gamershood.com/flashgames/4796
Living Room Escape
www.123bee.com/play/living_room_escape/4284.html
Mess Escape
www.escapegames24.com/2010/10/mess-escape.html
MOTAS
www.albartus.com/motas
The Bonte Room
home.scarlet.be/~bbonte/bonteroom.html
The Bonte Room 2
home.scarlet.be/~bbonte/bonteroom2.html
Thief 2
www.kongregate.com/games/Pastelgames/sneak-thief-2
Tucoga's Room
www.flonga.com/play/tucoga-s-room.htm

First person shooter (FPS)
Bioshock (c)
www.bioshockgame.com
Call of Duty
www.callofduty.com
Combat Arms (d)
en.combatarms.nexoneu.com/Intro.aspx
Free Online Games
first-person-shooter.freeonlinegames.name
Half-Life (c)
orange.half-life2.com
Sniper Aim
www.sniperaim.com

Hidden objects
Bedroom
kachbo.com/2010/11/hidden-objects-bedroom
Big Fish (d)
www.bigfishgames.com/download-games/genres/15/hidden-object.html
Dream Chronicles
www.playfirst.com/game/dreamchronicles
Energames
www.energames.com/games/online/hidden_object
Hidden Expedition
www.hiddenexpedition.com
iWin (d)
www.iwin.com/categories/games/hidden
Mystery Case Files
www.mysterycasefiles.com

Incentive
Chore Wars
www.chorewars.com
Epic Win (m)
www.rexbox.co.uk/epicwin
Plus One Me
www.plusoneme.com

Interactive fiction
Air Pressure
www.stoneagegames.com/games/2049/air-pressure
Choice of the Dragon
www.choiceofgames.com/dragon
Death in Sakkara
www.bbc.co.uk/history/interactive/games/death_sakkara
Hitchhiker's Guide (d)
h2g2remake.wordpress.com
Inanimate Alice
www.inanimatealice.com
Malinche (d)
www.malinche.net/freegames.html

Mobile
Angry Birds (m)
www.rovio.com
Bounty Island (m)
www.bountyislandgame.com
Galaxy on Fire (m)
www.galaxy-on-fire.com

Platform
Braid (d)
www.braid-game.com
Donkey Kong
www.donkeykonggame.net
Limbo (d)
www.limbogame.org
Little Big Planet (c)
www.littlebigplanet.com

Sonic the Hedgehog
www.freesonic.org
Super Mario Bros
www.onlinesupermario.com
Twang
www.nitrome.com/games/twang

Point and click
Blue Beanie
www.freeworldgroup.com/games8/gameindex/thebluebeanie.htm
City Tales
www.citytales.net
Droppy
www.pencilkids.com/the-vault/droppy-flash-game
Garfield
www.garfield.com/fungames/scavengerhunt/scavengerhunt.html
Gateway
www.mofunzone.com/online_games/gateway.shtml
Hamlet (d)
games.softpedia.com/get/Shareware-Games/Hamlet.shtml
Hamster Rescue
www.gamershood.com/flashgames/266
Indiana Jones (d)
store.steampowered.com/sub/2102/
Machinarium
machinarium.net
Nightmares
kids.aol.com/games/nightmares-episode-1
Ozzie (d)
www.acid-play.com/download/ozzie-and-the-quantum-playwright
Quest for the Rest
www.questfortherest.com
Scooby Doo
www.y8.com/games/Scooby_Doo_River_Rapids_Rampage
War Bears
www.gamegarage.co.uk/puzzle-games/warbears
Windowsil
gambolio.com/#/game-play:15876

Puzzle
Busta Brain
gambolio.com/#/game-play:29338
Boggle
www.fun-with-words.com/boggle.html
Bookworm
www.popcap.com/games/free/bookworm
Coded Hallway
www.bigfuntown.com/Game-1673.html

Crayon Physics (d)
www.crayonphysics.com
Gravity Stacker
www.freeonlinegames.com/
game/gravity-stacker.html
Orbox
www.gamebalance.com/games/
orbox.html
Tetris
www.freetetris.org
Text Twist
games.yahoo.com/game/
text-twist

Quiz
Blockbuster
www.teachers-direct.co.uk/
resources/quiz-busters
Buzz (c)
www.buzzthegame.com
The Image Quiz
www.gamesforthebrain.com/
game/imagequiz
Guesstimation
ninjawiki.com/games/Puzzle/
Play/Guesstimation.html
Impossible Quiz
www.impossible-quiz.com
Powerpoint Games (d)
jc-schools.net/tutorials/
PPT-games
Quiz Rocket
www.quizrocket.com
Space Quiz
www.prongo.com/space
Millionaire
www.dadt.com/millionaire

RPG
Amea
armorgames.com/play/
10487/amea
Castaway
armorgames.com/play/5885/
castaway
Drawn (d)
www.doublegames.com/
drawn-the-painted-tower.html
Epic Battle Fantasy
gambolio.com/#/
game-play:30317
Everquest II (d)
www.everquest2.com
Evony
www.evony.com
Fallout (c)
fallout.bethsoft.com
Final Fantasy (c)
www.finalfantasy.net
Freeware Games (d)
www.freewaregames.net

Lord of the Rings (d)
www.lotro.com
Runescape
www.runescape.com
Tibia
www.tibia.com
World of Warcraft (d)
battle.net/wow/en
Zelda (c)
www.zelda.com

Simulation
Ars Rendi
www.ars-regendi.com
Astro Empires
www.astroempires.com
Ayiti Cost of Life
ayiti.globalkids.org/game
Climate Challenge
www.bbc.co.uk/sn/hottopics/
climatechange/climate_challenge
Disaster Watch
www.christianaid.org.uk/
resources/games
Football Manager
www.onlinefootballmanager.co.uk
Fun PC Games (d)
www.funpcgame.com/1/5/
Simulation-Games.html
Hot Shot Business
disney.go.com/hotshot/hsb3
Peace Doves
nobelprize.org/educational/peace/
nuclear_weapons/game.html
The Sims (c)
www.thesims.ea.com
State of Debate
www.bbc.co.uk/schools/
ks3bitesize/game/english
Stop Disasters
www.stopdisastersgame.org
Third World Farmer
www.3rdworldfarmer.com
Virtual Villagers (d)
www.virtualvillagers.com

Singing and music
Lips (c)
www.lips.xbox.com
Karaoke
www.miniclip.com/games/karaoke
Karaoke Party
www.karaokeparty.com
Rock Band (c)
www.rockband.com
Sing Star (c)
www.singstar.com
Ultrastar (d)
www.ultrastargame.com

Sports
Driving
www.drivinggame.net
Driving Simulator
geoquake.jp/en/webgame/
DrivingSimulator
FIFA Soccer
www.ea.com/soccer/fifa
My Football Games
www.myfootballgames.co.uk
Tennis
www.tennisgame.net
Various (d)
www.brothersoft.com/games/
sports/
Wii Sports (c)
www.nintendo.com

Text adventure
Alter Ego
www.playalterego.com/alterego
Avalon
www.avalon-rpg.com/intro/
adventure.html
Colossal Cave
www.rickadams.org/adventure
Spent
playspent.org
Text Adventure
textadventure.wikia.com/wiki/
Start_of_game
Wake Up
www.textbasedadventure.com/1
Zork
thcnet.net/error/index.php

Virtual pet social sims
Animal Crossing (c)
www.animal-crossing.com
Adopt a Virtual Pet (d)
adopt-a-virtual-pet.cybercritters.
com/adoptavirtualpetonline/
catalog.php
Club Penguin
play.clubpenguin.com
Critter Forge
www.edgebee.com/games?id=2
Mara Pets
www.marapets.com
Moshi Monsters
www.moshimonsters.com
Pet Society
www.facebook.com/petsociety
Petville
petville.com
Shidonni
http://www2.shidonni.com
Virtual Pets
www.virtualpet.com/vp/links/
links.htm

Digital Play has so far argued on behalf of using computer games in the language classroom. We have provided an extensive explanation of the various types of game and the many, many games to be exploited. So what is the next step? To play.

Game on!

Before using digital play with your learners, *you* need to be suitably prepared – the more you know about games, the better you will be able to teach with them. And the more you know about what games your learners like, the more you'll find to inspire them when it comes to using games when practising language.

The non-connected classroom

It could be that in your teaching situation you can't play computer games with your learners in class. But not having access to a computer doesn't mean you can't engage in digital play – in the wider sense of the word –although the focus will be more on digital play *about* games rather than with games

The connected classroom

Let us suppose you have one computer in your classroom, connected to the internet and perhaps displaying the image through a projector to a large screen or an interactive whiteboard. With only one machine available, the challenge here is for the learners to get hands-on digital play experience – and for the teacher to avoid being the 'sage on the stage'.

Multiple connections

If you are lucky enough to have access to multiple computers then you have access to a huge degree of flexibility in what you can do with your learners to practise language through digital play. You could be using a class set of netbooks, laptops or tablets – or perhaps you have access to a computer room. Whatever, multiple connections mean multiple opportunities.

In Part B, then, we offer game plans for a bank of seriously playful – or playfully serious? – activities in three possible teaching scenarios. In Part C, we will be suggesting ways of integrating individual games into your syllabus, suggesting possible ways of accessing them for easy retrieval. For the moment, we simply highlight the *language skills* – listening, speaking, reading or writing – that are most prominently emphasised in each game.

Chapter One
Game On!

In this first chapter of Part B,
you will find a set of activities to get you started
and help you discover how best to motivate
your learners through digital games.

Try these out with your class first –
and let the game begin!

Game records

Figuring out the facts

○

The aim of the game
To show what the learners know about video games
with a quiz leading to a discussion

Ⓛ Ⓢ Ⓡ Ⓦ

Prepare to play

Prepare some quiz facts of your own – or use the examples opposite – and make a copy of the fact sheet for each learner.

Play

● Tell the learners you are going to test their knowledge of video games and ask them to work in groups or pairs.

● Give each learner a fact sheet and tell them there is a number missing from each fact.

● The learners read the facts and guess the missing number with a partner. Alternatively, you can give the learners the answers in the wrong order.
   • If they identify any unfamiliar vocabulary on the fact sheet, brainstorm the meaning together.
   • If they keep a vocabulary notebook, encourage them to write this vocabulary there.

● Read out the answers in order and ask the learners to listen and check/change their answers.

● Finish with a discussion about these facts and about video games in general. Here are some example prompts:
   • *Did any of the facts surprise you?* (Which ones?)
   • *Do you know any other facts?* (What are they?)
   • *How often do you play?* (Where? Who with?)
   • *Which games do you play?* (Which types?)

Play on

You should make sure you make a record of everything you learn for future classroom activities.

Meanwhile, your learners could research other fascinating facts themselves and prepare questions to quiz each other in subsequent lessons.

Answers a) 376   b) 1 million   c) 2 out of 5   d) 2,468
e) 214   f) 380 million   g) 200 million   h) 45.7 million
i) 49%   j) 100 million

Video game records

a) The most people dressed as a video game character:

On May 29th 2009, the MCM (Movie Comic Media) Expo was held in London and _____ people dressed up as their favourite video game character.

b) The fastest-selling Nintendo DS title:

The Nintendo DS (dual screen) version of Pokémon Platinum went on sale in Japan in September 2008 and it sold over _____ copies in the first two days.

c) The proportion of gamers in the US who are women:

Most video game playing is associated with boys or men but research suggests that _____ gamers are women.

d) The most money taken by a single arcade machine in a single week:

The most income taken by an arcade machine was $_____ in the US in one week in 1993.

e) The game soundtrack which contains the most number of licensed songs:

GTA (Grand Theft Auto) IV contains _____ licensed music tracks that can be heard while playing the game. The previous record holder was GTA: San Andreas, with 156 tracks.

f) The most successful movie franchise based on a video game:

The Resident Evil films have made more than $_____ .

g) The most successful game franchise:

The Mario video game series have sold over _____ copies worldwide.

h) The best-selling individual video game:

Wii Sports sold over _____ copies from between the time it was launched in 2006 to May of 2009.

i) The average age of a gamer:

In the US about 26% of gamers are over 50 years old, _____ are between 18 to 49 years old and 25% are under 18.

j) The best-selling PC video game series:

The life-simulation game called The Sims is the best-selling PC series in the world, with over _____ sold around the world.

Sources
1 *Guinness Book of Gamers' Records (2008–2010)*
2 *http://www.onlineeducation.net/videogame*

Devil's advocate

A digital debate

The aim of the game
To argue for and against computer games,
discussing the benefits and the dangers

(L) (S) (R) (W)

Top ten

The most popular games

The aim of the game
To discuss the merits of particular games
and choose a class 'Top Ten'

(L) (S) (R) (W)

Prepare to play

You may want to compile a list of typical arguments for and against playing computer games to share with your learners before you start this activity. You will find some of these in Part A. Alternatively, if the learners are advanced, you can find an article that mentions the subject.

Play

- Tell the learners that you are going to have a class debate to decide whether or not digital games should be banned. Ask for volunteers to speak 'for' and 'against' the motion – or *you* decide, and simply split the class into two.

- Ask each of the two halves to work in smaller groups and to write notes on why some people might suggest digital games should be banned (the violence in them can lead to real-life violence, etc) or why they should be promoted (they encourage hand–eye coordination, etc).

- Your learners will probably have lots of ideas of their own but, just in case, you may want to write some of *your* examples on the board – to get them started.

- Ask for a volunteer from each half to put the motion *for* and *against*, and then open the floor up for debate.

- Continue the discussion until you run out of time or until it reaches its natural conclusion.

- Ask everyone in the class to vote.

Play on

A good follow-up activity would be to ask the learners to write up their own personal opinions, based on what everyone said during the debate.

Prepare to play

Look for a 'Top Ten Games' list on one of the games sites or in an online newspaper, and copy out the titles and the reason for their inclusion in the list.

Play

- Ask the learners to choose their top three computer games and to write them down on a piece of paper or in their notebooks.

- Ask them to think about *why* they liked these games so much – they can write some notes if they wish.

- In groups of three or four, the learners talk about their favourite games and why they chose them. Then each group creates a list of the games, ranking them (number 1 being the best, number 2 the second best, etc) in order of preference.

- The learners form larger groups and compare their lists. If there are any differences, they discuss the merits of each game until they agree on the order.

- Next, ask them to read their lists aloud and hold a discussion at class level, taking votes to create a final list.

- Finally, compare the class list with the list you found earlier. What do they think of *your* list?

Play on

If the learners are engaged by this, they can also create another list, the 'Bottom Ten' – their list of the worst games they have ever played.

Make sure you keep a record of their tastes in games, not only the one they like – but also the ones they don't.

Game survey

What's your game?

The aim of the game
To talk about the games the learners play –
so you can use these games in class

Prepare to play

Make photocopies of survey questions A and B (opposite)
for all your learners.

Play

- Give out the surveys and ask the learners to ask each
  other the questions in pairs and make a record of their
  partner's answer.

- After completing the survey, the learners report back
  to the class, sharing any surprising answers or unusual
  information.

- As the games are mentioned, write them on the board
  in no particular order. When the learners have finished
  reporting the results of the survey, ask them about the
  games now listed on the board:
  - *Which game do most people think is the best?*
  - *Who is the most popular game character?*
  - *Which game console do most people in the class use?*

- Next, ask the learners to write their own answers to the
  questions they asked their partner.

- Finally the learners write a paragraph about the results,
  comparing them with their own answers to the question
  (eg *Jon likes puzzle games, but I prefer football ones*).

- Collect their work.

Play on

You can use the information in the work they handed in
to hold a discussion on their comparative tastes, as well as
reviewing for accuracy the language they used.

Be sure to take careful note of your learners' preferences –
both from their written work and the discussion – for future
classroom activities.

Video game survey

Student A

*Work with a partner and ask and answer the following
questions. Make a note of the answers.*

1 When did you first play a video game?
2 When did you last play a video game?
3 What was the first game you ever played?
4 What is your favourite game machine/console?
5 What is your favourite game?
6 What is your least favourite game?
7 What was the last game you actually finished?
8 What was the most difficult game you have ever
   played?
9 Who is your favourite video game character?

Video game survey

Student B

*Work with a partner and ask and answer the following
questions. Make a note of the answers.*

1 Do you like playing video games? Why? Why not?
2 When do you usually play games?
3 Where do you usually play games?
4 Who do you usually play games with?
5 Who in your family plays the most games?
6 How often do you play video games?
7 How often do you buy new games?
8 What types of game do you prefer?
9 What types of game do you never play?

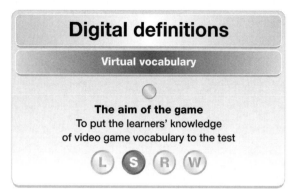

Digital definitions

Virtual vocabulary

The aim of the game
To put the learners' knowledge
of video game vocabulary to the test

L S R W

Prepare to play

Prepare a list of game vocabulary suitable for your class – or use one of the lists opposite.

Play

- Tell the learners that you have made a list of ten words about video games. These could be words that have occurred in any previous activities you might have done.

- Ask the learners to work in teams and guess what they are, writing them down on a sheet of paper.

- The teams take it in turn to call out the words from their lists.
  - To add an element of fun, a point is awarded to the team that guesses one of the words on your list first.
  - If a team calls out a word that isn't on your list, write it on the board.

- When they have finished calling out their words, write the remaining words on your list on the board.

- Next, ask the teams to take turns trying to define a word on the board, and award five points each time a team manages to come up with a good definition. For example:
  - *It's a device used to control a video game.* (controller)

- At the end of the activity, declare a winner. If there are any words left over, you can provide the definitions.

Play on

You can ask the learners to prepare further lists of words and definitions to ask each other in future lessons.

Basic game vocabulary

save   load   exit   select   click   download

console   controller   character   level

Suggested answers

save to store information about progress in a game

load to start playing a game from the last saved place

exit to finish a game

select to make a choice

click to push a button on the mouse

download to make a copy of a game on your own computer

console a special games machine you can connect to a TV

controller the device you use to control the actions of a character

character an imaginary person represented in a game

level a number that represents how well a character has progressed and the difficulty of a part of a game

---

Advanced game vocabulary

noob   frag   avatar   boss   bot   clan

fail   spawn   grinding   lag

Suggested answers

noob a completely new or inexperienced player

frag to kill an enemy with an explosive device

avatar the virtual character you control when playing a game

boss a powerful opponent in a game that a player must beat in order to finish a level

bot a non-player character controlled by the computer

clan a group of players who play together online

fail the act of losing a game in an embarrassing way

spawn the act of entering a game or starting a life in a game

grinding repeatedly performing an action in order to gain a level or achievement

lag when a poor internet connection causes an online game to slow down

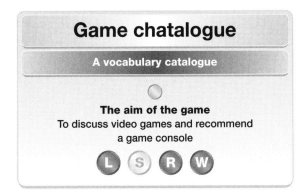

Game chatalogue

A vocabulary catalogue

The aim of the game
To discuss video games and recommend
a game console

L S R W

Prepare to play

Find some video game catalogues. Any store that specialises in games and gaming will probably have free catalogues of the latest games. Alternatively, find toy catalogues and bring to class the pages that feature video games (there will be quite a few!). The catalogues need not be in English.

Play

- If possible, organise the classroom so that you are all in a circle or semi-circle.

- Pass the game catalogues around. Let the learners look at the pictures and make comments (even in their own language, for the moment). Don't say anything yet.

- Express an interest yourself in the contents of the catalogues. If appropriate, you might tell the learners you are thinking of buying a console and some games for a family member who is their age.

- Respond with interest to any comments or suggestions that they make, trying to be as flexible and open as possible and encouraging 'chat'.
    - Use questions like the ones opposite to help keep the conversation going.
    - Don't correct the learners – unless you can't understand what they are saying.

- During the conversation, write any interesting vocabulary that comes up on the board. Later, refer to this language, eliciting the meaning and encouraging the learners to make a record of it in vocabulary notebooks.

- Once the learners have contributed to the conversation, bring it to a close by asking them again for their recommendations and why. At this point, you can reformulate any persistent language errors.

Play on

You can ask the learners to write up their suggestions in a letter to you. Give them the structure opposite to help them.

- What's the best console?
- What game do you recommend for me/my nephew/ niece/son/daughter?
- What video/console/computer games have you got?
- Do you know this game?
- Do you like this game?
- Why/why not?
- What do you do in this game?
- Which is the best game?

Dear (teacher),

If you are thinking of getting a console, we think you should get … because … .

Some good games to buy are … and … and … because … .

Don't buy … because … .

I am sure you will enjoy playing!

Yours,

GCAs

Game chat acronyms

The aim of the game
To write a dialogue together which includes typical game chat abreviations

(L) (S) (R) **W**

Prepare to play

Prepare a number of video game role situation cards – or photocopy the ones provided opposite – and bring some blank sheets of paper into class.

Play

- Write the following acronyms on the board:
  - *LOL*
  - *ROFL*
  - *BRB*

- Ask the learners where you can see them (in a game or in chat) and what they think they mean:
  - *laugh out loud*
  - *roll on floor laughing*
  - *be right back*

- Brainstorm more acronyms together and write them on the board. If the learners don't know any, then you can use some from the list opposite.

- Tell them they are going 'to chat' to each other as if they were online. Divide them into pairs of Student A and Student B and give them each a role card.

- Give the Student As the pieces of paper and ask them to start the chat, writing a response based on their role card. When they have finished, they should pass the paper to the Student Bs, who respond to what has been written.

- Ask the learners to keep 'chatting' for as long as they can, encouraging them to use the acronyms when appropriate.

- After ten minutes or so, stop them and let the learners read each other's chats.

- Finally, see how many of the acronyms they remember, awarding points to the learner who answers first.

Play on

You can use some of the pieces of paper as the basis of a test in class a few days later, asking the learners to identify what the acronyms mean.

Role situation 1

You are chatting during an online car racing game.

Student A: *You see something very odd happening to B's car.*

Student B: *You don't see anything.*

Role situation 2

You are playing a game together online.

Student A: *You have to go soon.*

Student B: *You want A to keep playing.*

Role situation 3

Student A: *You are learning a new game and asking B for advice.*

Student B: *You don't know how to play very well.*

Role situation 4

Student A: *You are chatting online and trying to persuade B to play your favourite game.*

Student B: *You would prefer to play a different game.*

GCAs

AFK – away from keyboard	*HTH* – hope this helps
ATM – at the moment	*TIA* – thanks in advance
BTW – by the way	*TTYL* – talk to you later
FYI – for your information	*OTOH* – on the other hand
THX – thanks	*NP* – no problem
IMO – in my opinion	*OMG* – oh my gosh!
IRL – in real life	*IGU* – I give up
CUL – see you later	

Chapter Two
The non-connected classroom

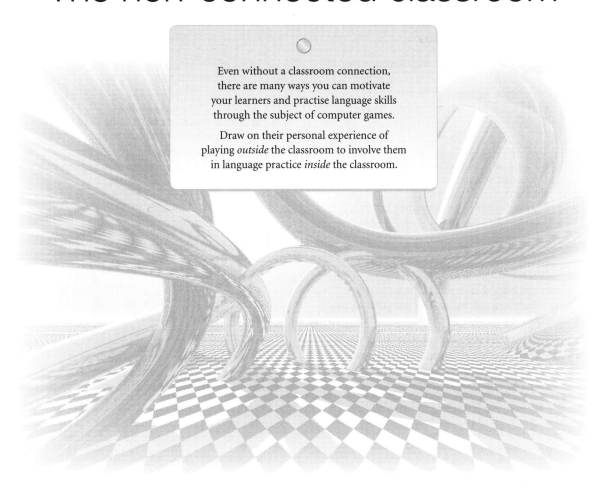

Even without a classroom connection, there are many ways you can motivate your learners and practise language skills through the subject of computer games.

Draw on their personal experience of playing *outside* the classroom to involve them in language practice *inside* the classroom.

It's not real!

Game world versus real world

The aim of the game
To compare the virtual world to the real world,
saying how real life is different

(L) (S) (R) (W)

Prepare to play

Think of a popular game world and write some sentences comparing what can be done there as opposed to the real world (see the example below). Make sure you mix the verbs you use: *can, can't, have to, don't have to, don't need to*, etc.

Pacman

You can't stay in one place for a long time.
You have to eat a lot of cherries to survive.
You have to run fast or you will be eaten.
You mustn't sleep.
You need to avoid lots of different-coloured ghosts.

Play

● Tell the learners you are going to read out some sentences about a game world that compare it to our world, and that you want them to listen carefully and guess which game you are talking about.

● When the learners have guessed, ask them to work in pairs and think of similar sentences about a different game world that they both know, using the same structures (eg *You can fly in the game, but you can't in real life*).

● In their pairs, the learners take turns to read out their sentences to see if their partners can guess the game. When they have finished, they change partners and read out their sentences again.

● While they are doing this, monitor and note down any examples you want to draw attention to.

● Finally, ask the learners to repeat the activity but – instead of using *can* and *can't*, etc – to compare different aspects of the worlds in other ways (eg *The game world is flat, but our world is 3D*).

Play on

The learners can think of their ideal game world, invent a name for it and write five sentences about it.

What game am I?

A game guessing game

The aim of the game
To answer questions about a game
and then quiz each other

(L) (S) (R) (W)

Prepare to play

Make copies of a 'What game am I?' worksheet (see the example below) for each learner.

What game am I?
Imagine you are inside the world of the game you have chosen. Answer the following questions:

1 I am _____ (*age*)
2 I look _____ (*adjective of physical description*)
3 I am wearing _____ (*clothes*)
4 It's _____ (*time of day*)
5 I am carrying _____ (*some of the things you have with you*)
6 I feel _____ (*adjective of feeling*)
7 I look around me and I see _____ (*description of the place*)
8 I have to _____ (*what you have to do*)
9 I can't _____ (*something you are not able to do*)
10 _____ (*one more clue*)

Play

● Tell the learners to choose a game – they are going to have to answer questions on it.

● Give them a copy of the worksheet, or dictate the sentences, and then ask them to complete the questions as best they can for the game they have chosen.

● The learners take turns reading out their sentences, to see who can guess the game first. Award a point to the one who guesses first. If nobody guesses, the point goes to the learner who asks the questions.

● Play until all the learners have had a turn, and then declare the winner.

Play on

You can ask the learners to tell you which of the statements were most helpful when guessing the game, and to think of other statements that would have made the guessing easier.

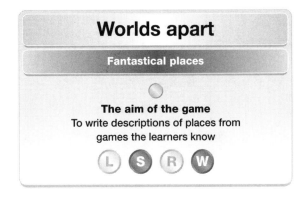

Day in, day out

Fantastical characters

The aim of the game
To write the daily routines and a personal description of a game character

Worlds apart

Fantastical places

The aim of the game
To write descriptions of places from games the learners know

Prepare to play

Write out some *Wh-* questions (including *How?*) for daily routines (or use the examples below).

- *What do you do?*
- *Where do you live?*
- *When do you get up?*
- *What do you usually do in the morning?*
- *What do you have for lunch?*
- *How do you spend your afternoons?*
- *What do you like to do in the evening?*
- *What do you do at the weekend?*

Play

- Ask the learners to tell you the names of game characters, and write these on the board. Stop when you have one per learner.

- Each learner chooses a name from the board, but keeps it a secret.

- Tell the learners you are going to read out some questions and they are to answer them as if they were the game character they have chosen.

- The learners listen to your questions and write the answers for their character in complete sentences. Remind them they have to keep the name a secret.

- When you have finished, ask them to take turns to read out the sentences for the other learners to guess the identity of their game character.

- Take note of any mistakes the learners make in their sentences – and deal with these at the end.

Play on

The learners can reformulate their sentences, turning them into a paragraph (in the third person this time) about their chosen game character. Ask them to mention the name of the character on this occasion and to add sentences if necessary, to make the paragraph more interesting.

Prepare to play

Find three or four screenshots of game worlds you think the learners will be familiar with (see the suggestions below). Choose images that focus on *place* rather than on *characters*.

- Super Mario Land
- Liberty City (*Grand Theft Auto*)
- Shambhala (*Uncharted 2*)
- Rivet City (*Fallout 3*)
- New Austin (*Red Dead Redemption*)
- Rapture (*Bioshock*)
- Halo landscape
- Twighlight Realm (*Zelda*)
- Azeroth (*World of Warcraft*)

Play

- Pin the images to the board (or use a data projector) and ask the learners to identify the games or the places.

- Choose one of the images and ask the learners: *What kind of a place is it?* Write adjectives next to the image. Prompt with questions as necessary (*Is it a safe or a dangerous place? Is it crowded? Is the forest a magic forest?*).

- Ask the learners to tell you the names of some other computer games they play or have played, and write the names on the board. Stop when you have 8–10 different game worlds.

- Ask the learners to think of one of the games and answer the same question: *What kind of a place is it?* Tell them to work with a partner and make a list of adjectives that could be used to describe the game world.

- In pairs, ask the learners to start expanding their lists of adjectives into sentences – and to combine the adjectives:
  - It is a dangerous, violent place.
  - It has great high mountains.

Help them with adjective order where necessary.

Play on

You can ask the learners to combine the sentences together to form a paragraph that describes the place of the game.

43

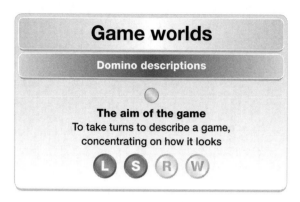

Game worlds

Domino descriptions

The aim of the game
To take turns to describe a game,
concentrating on how it looks

L S R W

Prepare to play

Prepare a description of a game world that you know, or use one of the examples opposite.

Play

- Read out a description of a game world and ask the learners to guess what game you are describing. If necessary, repeat with a second description.

- Tell the learners they are going to work in pairs and describe a game world to each other, as you did in your example. Now they have information about *two* game worlds (not including your examples).

- They change partners and describe their game world *and* the game world their partner told them about. Now they have information about *four* game worlds.

- They change partners again and describe to each other their game world and the three game worlds they have heard about. When they finish this round, they will have heard about *eight* game worlds.

- Finally, ask the learners to take turns to describe one of the worlds (not theirs) to the class. On the board, keep track of which ones have been described.

Play on

The learners can choose one of the game worlds they heard about that was *unfamiliar* to them and to write it up as a brief description.

Game worlds

Space Invaders

The world consists of four houses which you have to defend against an alien attack. The sky is black, so the attack happens at night, and you have a missile launcher which moves along the ground from left to right or right to left.

The aliens are very well organised in a rectangle and there are three different types. They also move from left to right, and also down towards you, firing at your houses and you as they do so. They move slowly at first and then speed up, which makes it difficult to shoot them.

If you destroy all of the aliens, then there's another wave of them to take their place. This continues until you run out of missile launchers!

Animal Crossing: City People

You move to a pretty village full of friendly people and buy a house from Tom Nook, who is the owner of the general store. The village is full of fruit trees, and you can earn money by collecting fruit and selling it to Mr. Nook. You can also go fishing and collect seashells to be able to pay off the mortgage on your new house.

With the money, you can buy furniture for your house or use it in the city to buy clothes or works of art. There are lots of people in the village you can meet and make friends with, visiting their houses and doing errands for them. The village changes with the seasons, so you will see snow in winter and it'll be bright and sunny in the summer.

Among the other places you can visit in the village, there's a museum with an observatory, a café where a musician plays every Saturday evening, and the town hall.

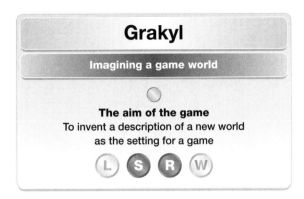

Grakyl

Imagining a game world

The aim of the game
To invent a description of a new world
as the setting for a game

L S R W

Prepare to play

Prepare a description of your own invented game world, or use the example opposite.

Play

- Ask the learners to think of a game world they know that they particularly liked, and ask them to say what it was about it that they liked.
  - Was it mysterious?
  - Did it have any strange plants or animals?

- Tell them they are going to work in groups of three or four and invent their own setting for a game.

- Read out your description, or the example opposite, to give them a better idea of what they have to do.

- Ask the groups to discuss together the elements of their game world and for one of the learners to act as secretary and take notes. As they do so, monitor and help them with any language they may need.

- Ask a volunteer from each group to give a mini-presentation of the game world and encourage the rest of the class to ask questions.

- Finally, the class can take a vote on the world they liked the best.

Play on

You can ask the learners to invent a computer game but, this time, they take what they consider to be the best elements from other games – a 'mashup'. They can limit themselves to just two or can choose from as many as they like.

They work in groups of three or four to discuss their games, following a similar procedure to *Grakyl* and finishing off with a class vote.

Grakyl

The game takes place on the lost island of Grakyl, which is in the middle of the South Pacific. A group of survivors of a plane crash find themselves on a deserted beach and seek shelter in a cave near a lake because of a strange green rain that falls from the sky and burns the skin.

The survivors find out that the rain occurs for five minutes at the same time every hour and so as they explore the island they must always find a place to go to take cover until it stops. As they move deeper into the interior of the island, the vegetation becomes stranger and they have to avoid or deal with giant man-eating plants.

What has caused these strange mutations?

Arriving at the volcano in the centre of the island, the survivors find a labyrinth of dark watery caves where they will discover the secret behind the island and also a way of getting back home.

Good, better, best

Character comparisons

The aim of the game
To describe and compare the personal
characteristics of computer game characters

Prepare to play

Identify a number of game characters that are well known to
the class (eg Supermario and Sonic the Hedgehog). Find an
image of each on the Web and bring them to class.

Play

- Present your pictures of game characters to the learners
  and check what they know about them. Where possible,
  get the learners to explain features of the characters.
  Feed in language as needed, eliciting physical and mental
  characteristics such as *strength, weight, height, speed,
  intelligence*, etc.

- Write on the board the nouns and elicit some adjectives
  that go with each one:

strength	*strong*
weight	*heavy*
intelligence	*intelligent*
height	*tall*
speed	*fast*

Round One

- Erase the adjectives and draw a line next to each noun.

- Split the class into several teams and allocate each one a
  game character. Explain that each character has a total
  of 100 points. These points must be distributed over the
  characteristics, however the team likes. Set a time limit.

- When the learners have finished, ask one representative
  from each team to come and write up their character's
  name and characteristics with the number-values next
  to each one. You should have complete columns, one for
  each character. Make sure the numbers add up to 100.

- Begin asking questions, reminding the learners of
  the adjective form (including the comparatives and
  superlatives). For example: *So, who's stronger? Who's the
  strongest?*

- Elicit the answer, then continue with the other
  characteristics.

- Ask the learners: *Who's better?* or *Who's the best?* Allow
  any answer, as long as they can justify it with reference to
  the characteristics they mentioned.

- Now ask the learners, individually, to create four
  sentences comparing the characters, using the
  characteristics above: *Supermario is stronger than Sonic
  the Hedgehog.* Tell them that three of these sentences
  must be true and one must be false.

- In pairs, the learners read each other's sentences and
  decide which one is false, consulting the characteristics
  on the board.

Round Two

- You can line chairs up in facing rows and get the learners
  to sit down opposite each other. Ask them to each choose
  a different charater.

- Call out: *The strongest is the winner!* Each player has to
  say the number recorded next to 'strength'. Whoever has
  the highest number for this character is the winner, and
  gets a point.

- They should remember to keep a record of their points.

- The learners now stand up and move, so they are facing
  a new partner. Call out a different characteristic, eg *The
  fastest is the winner!* If the score is the same nobody
  gets a point (ie if they have the same character on this
  occasion).

- Continue this way, alternating characteristics each time,
  until the learners have all sat opposite each other.

- Ask which learners have the most points: *Who's the
  winner?*

Play on

The learners choose another, different character and prepare
to play in the next lesson, allocating points for each adjective
(from a total of 100) as before. Next class, the game is played
again but, this time, with the learners' characters, instead of
your characters.

Power wishes

If only ...!

The aim of the game
To discuss the abilities of game characters, choosing three special powers the learners would like to have

Prepare to play

Prepare some sample cards (see the examples opposite) with the name of a popular game character and their special powers written on them.

Play

○ Tell the learners you have selected some popular game characters, and ask them to guess who they are by asking you *yes/no* questions about their special abilities (*Can she fly? Is he very strong?* etc).

○ Ask the learners to secretly think of another game character and what they can do. Give each learner a slip of paper and ask them to write the name of the character at the top and some of the things the character can do (as in the examples opposite).

○ Take in the slips of paper and shuffle them.

○ Now ask the learners to secretly choose three special abilities or powers that they would like to have, and to write them down on another slip of paper in the form of a wish (*I wish I had wings*, etc).

○ Give each learner one of the slips of paper with the name of a game character and their special powers, and tell them to keep it secret. Tell them they have the power to grant any wishes that their card-character has. However, they cannot grant *themselves* a wish.

○ The learners move around the class telling people their wishes, until they find someone who can grant them. The winner is the first learner who does one of the following:
    1 makes all three of their wishes come true
    2 grants three wishes

Play on

For homework, the learners invent a name and write a description of a new game character that has these three powers/abilities – to share with everyone next class.

Sonic the Hedgehog

can ...
run at supersonic speed
turn into a ball to attack

has ...
super strength
a flexible body

Mario

can ...
jump very high
grow very large
shrink in size

has ...
many lives

Prince of Persia

can ...
climb very high
travel through time
turn invisible

is ...
an expert sword fighter

Lara Croft

can ...
solve puzzles

is ...
athletic
very intelligent
an expert fighter

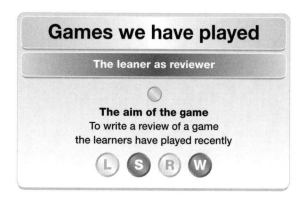

Games we have played

The leaner as reviewer

The aim of the game
To write a review of a game
the learners have played recently

Prepare to play

Make copies of the game reviews opposite for every two learners in the class. Alternatively, you can find examples of reviews of current games on the internet, using the search term: (name of game) + review.

Play

- Ask the learners to think of a game they have played recently and to write notes about what they liked and what they didn't like about it.

- Show them the model reviews you have prepared, and ask them to note the content and style of the writing. Draw their attention to different features of the review (in bold in our examples).

- Ask the learners to plan their review and then to talk about it to a partner.

- They write their reviews. When they finish:
  - Student A reads out their review to Student B as if they were talking on a radio programme.
  - Student B has to listen and then ask at least one question about the game when Student A has finished reading.

  They then reverse roles.

- Ask the learners to change partners a few times – and repeat.

Play on

You can publish the reviews in a class blog or wiki, or pin them to the walls and ask the class to add their own classification (a mark out of ten) to each of them. Do they agree with the reviewer?

Game reviews

Pro Evolution Soccer 3D

If you want to impress your friends, show them this football game. **The first time you experience** the 3D, it will leave you with your mouth open. **The only problem with the game is that**, apart from the 3D, it's the same old game.

Classification: 6/10

Nintendogs + Cats

The object of this game is to look after virtual dogs and cats. **You can also** teach the pets to do tricks. **Playing this game is** relaxing. **Unfortunately, there is no** real aim to the game, so you won't be playing it for long.

Classification: 5/10

Red Dead Redemption

This is an exciting action game. **It is set in** the Wild West. **You play** a gunman looking for someone from your past. **There are** lots of missions. **You have to** travel around on your horse and help people. **The result is** impressive.

Classification: 9/10

My favourite game

The learner as poet

The aim of the game
To write a poem by following instructions in a part dictation/part creative-writing activity

(L) (S) (R) (W)

Prepare to play

Make sure the learners have pens and paper – that's all they need!

Play

- Tell the class you are going to help them write about one of their favourite computer games, and they should get ready to write and follow your instructions.

- If you feel it necessary, use the example poems opposite to show them what they will be doing. You can read the poems and ask the learners to guess the game that is being described.

- Give the learners a minute to think about a computer game they really like and why they like it.

- Now ask them to follow your instructions – see the 'Poem procedure' opposite.

- If you ask the learners to leave out the name of the game, it turns the subsequent reading of the poem into a guessing game, which can be fun.

- When they have finished, tell the learners they have written a poem!

- They should add and change anything they want, to improve it, while you help them with the changes. Then they read them out to each other or to the whole class.

- Collect the poems and publish them in a booklet. This works even better if you have several classes writing poems.

- Hold a competition to decide the best title for this little book of poems and for the design of the cover.

Play on

If this activity goes down well, you can repeat it but, this time, ask the learners to think of a game they really *don't* like – they simply add negatives where appropriate. Add these poems to the book.

Poem procedure

- You write up the first line, beginning:
  This is the game that makes me ...
  The learners add a suitable ending (verb/adjective).

- You write up the second line, beginning:
  The one where/which/that ...
  The learners briefly describe what happens in the game.

- Begin the next line:
  You ...
  They add some verbs that describe details of the game.

- Continue with another detail of the game by writing:
  And ...
  The learners complete the next line.

- Begin the next line:
  Because ...
  The learners write a continuation.
  They can add another *Because* line if they want.

- Start the penultimate line:
  At the end of the game ...
  Everyone should write what happens.

- Finish the poem by writing:
  And ... or *But ...*
  The learners add their own ideas.

My favourite game

This is the game that makes me feel alive
The one where I sing with the stars
You try to be better each time you play
Because the name of the game is fame
At the end of the game I have no voice
But I love it even though I am tired.
(*SingStar* – by Carla, age 18)

This is the game that makes me laugh
The one which looks like real life
You walk and talk and cook and clean
And work and make friends and eat pizza
Because that's what you have to do
The end of the game never arrives
But I'm happy because it's so cool.
(*The Sims* – by Judith, age 13)

The name of the game

Game name poems

The aim of the game
To use favourite digital games
to write an acrostic poem

(L) (S) (R) (W)

Prepare to play

Prepare a poem based on the title of a computer game that the learners will know (or use the example below).

Facing almost	The hero's **F**ight leads to
Impossible tasks on	**A** series of
Nearly	**N**ightmarish
Alien	**T**asks
Landscapes.	**A**nd
	Several
	Years pass before the end is in sight.

Play

- Using your own example or the one above, write the title of the computer game on the board plus words associated with it, then show the learners how you can take these words to create an acrostic poem.

- Ask the learners to think of the title of their favourite computer game and to brainstorm associated vocabulary.

- They write the name of their chosen game vertically down the left-hand side of a page. They then write a sentence/parts of a sentence with each letter of the word, using some of the vocabulary associated with that computer game – and create their own poem.

- Monitor, and help the learners with any language difficulties that they may have.

- When they have finished, the learners can decorate the page with drawings or pictures from the game. Then, together, make a wall display in the classroom and invite another class to come to the game-poem exhibition.

Play on

The learners can write another poem for homework, and to write a paragraph explaining why they chose this game and what it is about it they like so much.

There and back

Two-way translations

The aim of the game
To translate text into the learners' own language
then retranslate it back into English

(L) (S) (R) (W)

Prepare to play

Find and print a copy of a short walkthrough (or use the example below) for each pair of learners in the class. You'll also need another copy of the walkthrough for each learner – for homework – and a class set of bilingual dictionaries.

Mystery Of Time And Space (MOTAS)

Stage 1
- Get the key from under the pillow.
- Open the locker and get the screwdriver out of the box.
- Put the wall poster under the door.

Stage 2
- Use the screwdriver to take the elephant picture off the wall.
- You'll get a thin screw.
- Use the thin screw on the door lock.

MOTAS: http://www.albartus.com/motas

Play

- Hand out the dictionaries and explain to the learners that they are going to translate the instructions (the walkthrough) for an online game into their own language.

- Ask them to work with a partner, and hand out one walkthrough to each pair.

- The learners use the dictionaries and translate the instructions into their own language in their notebooks. When they have finished, collect the walkthrough.

- Ask the learners to translate their translations back into English. When they have finished, give them the original walkthrough and ask them to compare what's written there with their translation. How accurate were they?

Play on

You can ask the learners to do the same at home but, this time, to use automatic translation software (such as *http://translate.google.com*) and see if the results are better.

Click change

Quick vocabulary transformation

The aim of the game
To rewrite the walkthrough for a game,
changing the word 'click' for different verbs

Prepare to play

Find a walkthrough of a game which overuses 'click on' (see the example opposite). Play the game yourself, replacing it in the walkthough with alternative verbs appropriate to the level of the class.

Play

- Write the name of the online game on the board, telling the learners that the objective of the game is to 'escape the room' and asking if they have played this type of game before.
  - Tell them that sometimes when playing these games people look for game guides ('walkthroughs') to help them solve the puzzles because they are often very difficult.
  - Tell them you have found instructions for this online game, but the instructions are written for someone using a computer.

- Ask the learners to help you change these verbs so that they are more like regular instructions for the character in the game. Before you begin, you may feel it appropriate to pre-teach some of the key words in the walkthrough you have chosen.

- Start dictating the sentences in the walkthrough one by one and give the learners time (in pairs or individually) after dictating each one to think of replacement verbs.

- When you have finished dictating, tell them the verbs you have as answers, but say that you will accept any alternative answers you all think make sense.

- Award the learners a point for each correct English word and declare the learner(s) with the most points the winner.

Play on

You can suggest the learners play the game with their walkthroughs for homework just for fun – and to revise the vocabulary at the same time.

The Bonte Room 2

Replace *Click on* in the walkthrough below with another verb.

1 *Click on* the coin on the top of the yellow picture of the bird.
2 *Click on* the ruler on the blackboard.
3 *Click on* the ruler on the bottom of the fireplace to get the wire.
4 *Click on* the screws on the fan with the coin.
5 *Click on* the metal grid.
6 *Click on* the wire with the fan to get a sharp point.
7 *Click on* the fan with the ruler.
8 *Click on* the chip card.
9 *Click on* the chip card in peanut machine.
10 *Click on* the peanuts.
11 *Click on* the sharp wire on the cactus.
12 *Click on* the peanuts on the cactus milk.
13 *Click on* the peanuts again.
14 *Click on* the first then the second rectangular buttons on the fireplace.
15 *Click on* the red button then the third and second rectangular buttons.
16 *Click on* the red button and then the first rectangular button.
17 *Click on* the metal grid in the fireplace (above the flames).
18 *Click on* the peanuts on the metal grid.
19 *Click on* the roasted peanuts again.
20 *Click on* the bird with the roasted peanuts.

http//:home.scarlet.be/~bbonte/bonteroom2.html

Suggested answers

1 find / pick up / get	11 jab / poke / use
2 take / pick up	12 put / place
3 use / poke	13 take / get
4 unscrew / remove	14 turn on / switch on
5 take off / remove	15 turn on / switch on
6 cut / slice	16 turn on / switch on
7 stop	17 put / place
8 get	18 place / put
9 put	19 get
10 press	20 feed

A game in 50 words

Mini-saga summaries

The aim of the game
To tell each other about games the learners have played and write them in the form of a mini-saga

(L) (S) (R) (W)

Prepare to play

Write a mini-saga (a short summary of exactly 50 words) of a game that you know, or use the example below.

> A group of birds are not very happy. A number of green pigs have stolen their golden eggs and refuse to return them. The birds decide to go after the pigs and, using catapults, they launch themselves at the home of the pigs, killing them and rescuing their golden eggs.
> (*Angry Birds*)

Play

- Read the text you have written (or the example above) and ask the learners to guess the game (*Angry Birds*).

- Ask the learners in pairs to think of a game they have both played that has a story.

- One learner starts to tell the story of the game, while the other takes notes. They then alternate until they are both happy they have covered the basics of the game.

- When the story is over, the learners take a look at their notes and add details that may have been missed.

- Next, tell the learners that they are to write up their notes and turn them into a 50-word synopsis of the game, using only the most important parts of the story and not including the title.

- When they have finished, ask the learners to read their stories aloud to the rest of the class without saying the name of the game. The others guess the game that the story is about.

Play on

At home, the learners can play the game their story was about and then write another summary, increasing the word count of the story to 100 words.

A game in 20 words

Be brief!

The aim of the game
To write game descriptions, read them out and guess each other's games

(L) (S) (R) (W)

Prepare to play

Prepare a few short descriptions of games (of 20 words) that the learners will know, or use the ones below. The descriptions should not contain the name of the games.

> You move into a new house, find a job and start making friends. You need to learn lots of things.
> (*The Sims*)
>
> You are a musician and go on tour with your band, playing gigs and earning money if you play well.
> (*Rock Band*)

Play

- Start with a 'dictogloss' of one of the descriptions you have prepared: tell the learners that you are going to read a short description of a computer game and they are to listen carefully then, after you have finished, they should try to recreate exactly what you said.

- When the learners have finished, ask them to compare what they have written with a partner, and then write the description on the board to compare. Can they guess what game it is?

- Tell them you are going to read out some other examples of computer games and, this time, just ask the learners to guess the games. Next, ask them to guess how many words were used in the descriptions.

- Tell the learners to think of a game they know and to write a description, using approximately 20 words.

- When they finish, they read the description to their partner, who has to guess. Ask the learners to change partners and repeat this a few times.

- Finally, ask them which games were easiest to guess – why?

Play on

You can ask the learners to increase the descriptions to 50 words, adding adjectives and other details about their games.

Game, set and match

Brainstorming battle

The aim of the game
To produce a list of the vocabulary sets
used in specific games

(L) (S) (R) (W)

Prepare to play

Prepare some slips of paper, and a list of 6–10 popular
computer game titles to use in class as examples (*Tetris,
Singstar, Fifa, Final Fantasy*, etc).

Play

- Divide the learners into teams of three or four. Each team
brainstorms game titles for the other teams, taking it
in turn to suggest a title. Write up the titles in different
columns for each team. Stop when you have about four
or six for each team.

- Check that at least someone from each team is familiar
with the games that have been chosen for them. If they
don't know a game, give them the choice to replace it
with one of the games that *you* wrote down before class.

- Next, ask the teams to write down on a piece of paper
as many words as possible associated with their team's
games. Tell the learners they have ten minutes to do
this. Meanwhile, write the title of each game on a slip of
paper, mix them up and divide them equally between the
teams.

- Someone from each team then takes it in turn to talk
about one of the computer games in their pile, choosing
one of the slips of paper but without mentioning the
name of the game. If there's a game they do not know,
they can choose a different slip of paper. The other
teams listen, and when they hear one of the words they
wrote down they tick it. They tick the word each time it
is repeated. Continue until each team has described the
games on their slips of paper.

- Finally, ask each team to add up the ticks and award them
a point for each one. Declare a winning team.

Play on

A good follow-up activity would be to hold a class discussion
about the games. Which is their favourite? Which game was
most difficult/easy to think of words for?

In the game

Applying for a part in a game

The aim of the game
To write a job application and go for a job interview
for a part in a particular game

(L) (S) (R) (W)

Prepare to play

Prepare a short application letter for the position of a
famous character in a game. See the Pacman example below
(*http://www.playpacmanonline.net*).

> Dear Game Designer,
>
> *I am writing to apply for the hero's job in your computer
> game. I am fast-moving, good at directions and I am also
> very good at avoiding ghosts.*
>
> *I like eating fruit and diamonds and I'm not afraid to chase
> ghosts if I see that they are scared and running away.*
>
> *I am available for an interview at your convenience. I look
> forward to hearing from you.*
>
> *Yours sincerely,*

Play

- Tell the learners that a job in a computer game is available
and you have applied for it. Dictate the application letter
and ask the learners to write the name of the computer
game character at the bottom. Confirm the identity.

- Give out the letter and ask the learners to underline the
useful language that will help them write their own job
application letter.

- In pairs, they write an application letter for a computer
game position, using your example as a model. Remind
them they must leave the name blank at the bottom.

- The learners put their job application letters up on the
classroom wall. They get up, read them and write the
name of a computer game character at the bottom.

- The learners look at the job application letter *they* wrote
and tick the names at the bottom if they are correct.

Play on

The learners can roleplay the interview that takes place
between the game designer and the game character.

Complaint to the enemy

Could you possibly ...?

The aim of the game
To write an email of complaint from the hero
of a game to their enemy

(L) (S) (R) **(W)**

Prepare to play

Ask the learners to work in pairs and to think of a game they both know well (Nintendo's *Mario* series, for example) that features a hero and an enemy (or enemies) – and to add each of these as the headers of two columns on a sheet of paper (eg Mario – Bowser).

Play

- Tell the learners to brainstorm things that the enemy does to make the hero's life difficult in a game, and to write these as sentences:
  - *Bowser breathes fire.*
  - *He grows to giant size.*
  - *He kidnaps Princess Peach.*

- Ask the learners how they would ask the enemy politely to stop doing these things, and elicit examples, writing them on the board:
  - *I would like you to stop breathing fire.*
  - *I'd prefer it if you'd not grow so big.*
  - *I wish you would go somewhere else.*

- Tell them they are now going to write a formal email from the hero of their game to the enemy, complaining about these things and asking them to stop.

- Start by asking them how to begin writing an email, and guide them through the opening paragraph (*Dear Bowser, I am writing to you today* ... etc).

- Ask the learners to politely complain to their enemy about the problems they took note of earlier.

- Help them finish their emails by signing off appropriately (*Kind regards, Mario*, etc).

Play on

Once the emails are written, you can give them to different learners and ask them to write replies from the enemy to the hero for homework. Make sure that the learners receive emails written from heroes of games they know, asking them to politely refuse to cooperate with the hero of the game.

Dear Kratos ... Love, Lara

From character to character

The aim of the game
To write informal letters from the point of view
of a game character

(L) (S) (R) **(W)**

Prepare to play

Think of two game characters that all your learners will know, to use as examples.

Play

- Tell the learners to choose two game characters, preferably from different games (eg Kratos from *God of War* and Lara Croft from *Tomb Raider*).

- Ask the learners to think of a typical 'day in the life' of one of the game characters and to write some notes about what they have done recently.

- Tell them that they are shortly going to be writing an informal letter from this character (eg Lara) to the other one (Kratos) and they should also think of some questions to ask them:
  - *How are things in Sparta?*
  - *Is it true you've just got a new tattoo?*

- Ask the learners to continue planning the letters and decide why they are writing to the other character (eg to invite them to join them on an adventure, to ask them for help with a puzzle in the game, etc). Help the learners decide how many paragraphs they are going to write and what the theme of each paragraph will be, and get them to produce a plan.

- Ask them to work in groups of three or four, and to explain their plans to each other. The others listen and suggest changes.

- They all write their letters and then exchange them with a partner. Finally, working in pairs, they take turns roleplaying a meeting between the characters.

Play on

A follow-up letter could be written by the learners, in their character-role, replying to the letter or responding to the recent meeting.

Wish you were here

Having a great time!

The aim of the game
To write postcards from a game character
to someone in the class

Prepare to play

Write a postcard from a game character (or use the example below) to demonstrate the informal letter-writing style used.

Dear Sonic,

How are you? I'm in Hyrule, taking a break from stealing the Chaos Emeralds. Link from the Legend of Zelda invited me to stay with him. He's a lot of fun.

We've been spending time riding horses and exploring the countryside. Princess Zelda has gone missing again, but I promise it had nothing to do with me!

Wish you were here.

Doctor Eggman

Play

◉ Ask the learners if they, or anyone they know, ever write postcards – When do they do it? What do they write?

◉ Read out your example postcard and ask the class if they know the computer game these characters come from. Brainstorm what other game characters would write about if they sent someone a postcard and write ideas up.

◉ Tell the learners that they are going to write a postcard from a game character to someone in the class (you decide who, so everyone is writing to someone) and they should choose a game character they know well.

◉ The learners write notes, and you help them correct or improve the language. Give them postcard-size pieces of paper or card and ask them to write their postcards.

◉ 'Send' the postcards to the recipients – if there's enough time and interest, they can write replies.

Play on

You can ask the learners to write another postcard for homework. This time, tell them that the character is having a terrible time and wishes they *weren't* there!

Up for sale

Writing classified ads

The aim of the game
To write a classified 'For Sale' advert
on behalf of a game character

Prepare to play

Prepare a description of an object for sale by a famous computer game character for your learners to read and guess the game and/or the character, or use the examples below.

Classified ad placed by Cloud Strife
from the 'Final Fantasy' series of games

For sale
Large yellow flightless bird that can be ridden. Good condition. One previous owner. Contact CS in Midgar for more information.

Classified ad placed by Sackboy
from the 'Little Big Planet' game

For sale
Large bag full of colourful stickers, costumes, materials, decorations and tools. Very useful collection for all sorts of platforms. Please contact SB of LBP.

Play

◉ Write your classified ads on the board and ask the learners to guess where they might see these (newspaper, magazine, website). Tell them that they were written by game characters and ask them if they can guess the name of the game and/or the characters who wrote them.

◉ Tell the learners that they are going to work in pairs and think of another computer game character and something they might want to sell. They write a classified ad, using the examples on the board as models and copying classified ads writing genre.

◉ The learners read out their classified ad for the rest of the class to guess the character and/or the computer game.

Play on

The learners can act out a roleplay where they ring each other up and ask about the items offered for sale.

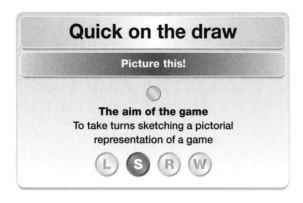

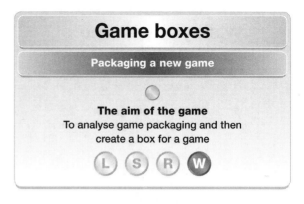

Quick on the draw

Picture this!

The aim of the game
To take turns sketching a pictorial representation of a game

Game boxes

Packaging a new game

The aim of the game
To analyse game packaging and then create a box for a game

Prepare to play

Prepare a list of games your learners will know, or ask *them* to do this before you play. Write the names of the games on slips of paper.

Play

- Choose a slip of paper at random and ask for a volunteer to start drawing.

- Show the volunteer the name of the game and ask them to draw it on the board. As the volunteer is drawing, they answer *yes* or *no* to the questions that the other learners might have – it is better to ask them to put their hands up and you pick them one by one.

- Ask the learners to guess what the game is, or to ask for clues. They must ask using the *yes/no* question format, or the questions and guesses will not be accepted:
  - *Is it a puzzle game?*
  - *Can more than one person play it?*
  - *Do you play it on a console?*

- The person who guesses comes up to the board to draw another game. Continue for a few minutes.

- While playing, take a note of the questions they ask, especially any that are incorrectly formed. When you finish the game, write some of these questions on the board and correct them together.

Play on

You can ask the learners to work in groups and find out which games were unfamiliar to some of the learners. Ask those who know these games to give a mini-presentation about the game to the group.

Prepare to play

If you can get hold of some actual game boxes, then this will work better. If not, images of game packaging can be easily found on the internet. Find a selection, and copy and paste them together on a couple of pages as examples.

Play

- Show the examples of packaging to the learners, and ask them to talk about the design and the way the games are described on the front and back of the boxes.

- Get the learners to decide on the common elements that all game boxes have (title/blurb/game genre/etc) by examining the examples in detail.

- Tell the learners they are going to invent their own game and the packaging to go with it. First of all they should decide what kind of game it is going to be (*game genre*) and then think of a *theme* and a *title*.

- They next write a short description of the game, based on the examples, for the back of the box and decide what pictures the packaging will show (writing a one-sentence description for each one).

- When everyone has finished, the game packaging can be displayed on the walls of the classroom.

Play on

A further, more detailed description can be produced by following the steps for *Game blurbs* on page 57.

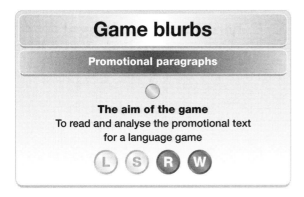

Game blurbs

Promotional paragraphs

The aim of the game
To read and analyse the promotional text
for a language game

L S **R** **W**

Prepare to play

Search the internet to find a 'blurb' of a recent game you think the learners will know (or use the example opposite, simplified and adapted from Nintendo's *Super Mario 64*). You may want to simplify the language, depending on the level of the learners.

Play

- Write the word *blurb* on the board and ask the learners if they know what it means ('brief promotional description that is found on the cover of a book, computer game', etc).

- Show the learners your example and ask them if they can guess the game. If they have played the game, ask them to tell you if the blurb is accurate.

- Look at the parts of the blurb together (the title, the slogan, the description) and deal with the meaning of any words or expressions the learners are unfamiliar with.

- Ask the learners to divide the parts of the text into the different parts of a table like the one opposite, writing the elements that talk about specific aspects of the game.

- Then, working in pairs, they think of another game they know and write in a similar table sentences that describe the *description*, *story* and *gameplay*.

- Afterwards, they use the sentences they have written to write a complete blurb for the game, adding a *title* and a *slogan*, as in your example.

- Finally, the learners read their blurbs aloud, without mentioning the title, and the others guess the games. Take note of any language that could be improved – to deal with at the end.

Play on

The learners can find the original blurbs (using the internet) and bring them to the next class – to compare them with what they wrote.

It's me, in 3D!
The first great 3D platform game

One bright, sunny day in Mushroom Kingdom, Mario goes to visit the princess, but when he arrives at her castle, there's nobody at home. Jumping through the pictures hanging from the walls, Mario moves through 15 magical worlds looking for 120 Power Stars stolen by the evil Bowser. The game world is a giant obstacle course, with 30 different types of enemies, hidden items and lots of puzzles to solve. Take advantage of all of Mario's abilities, including running, jumping, swimming and punching – he can even perform a backward somersault! – and collect the special bonuses to give him short-lived powers, including the ability to fly.

Super Mario 64 is a stunning adventure
in a spectacular 3D world.

Description

eg *A bright, sunny day*

Story

eg *Mario goes to visit the princess.*

Gameplay

eg *Collect the 120 Power Stars.*

Promotional language

eg *Take advantage of ...*

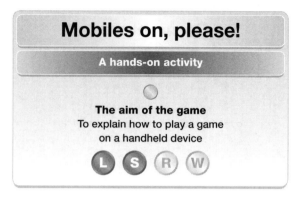

Prepare to play

You may want to use some pictures of typical game consoles (PlayStation 3, Xbox 360, Nintendo Wii, PlayStation Portable (PSP), Nintendo DS, etc) to facilitate the discussion.

Play

- Write the following questions on the board and ask the learners to talk in small groups about games consoles:
  - *Do you own a games console? Which one(s)?*
  - *What do you like/dislike about it/them?*
  - *What other games consoles do you know/like?*
  - *What are the advantages/disadvantages of each?*
  - *What feature(s) would you like on a new one?*

- After five or ten minutes, depending on how things are going, stop the learners and find out what they thought.

- Tell them that they are going to work in groups and design their own game console for the future, and that they can make it have any features they want.

- As they write, ask a group secretary to take notes on what is decided, writing a *specification sheet* (a list of bullet points of features).

- When the group think they have enough information, they should review the contents of the specification sheet and add/remove anything they feel necessary.

- Next, tell them they are to use the specification sheet to work on a *sales description* of the console. At this point they should also give it a name and think of a *slogan*.

- Finally, the learners give a mini-presentation to the class, comparing their invented game console to one of the existing ones, saying what the differences are.

Play on

The learners could produce a poster of the console on paper, or they could use a digital poster-creating website such as *http://www.glogster.com*. They can draw it, and add the written description and slogan.

Prepare to play

Make sure the learners bring their mobile phones/iPods to class as they will be needing them. Every learner will need a handheld device which has a game on it. This could be a mobile phone, an iPod or similar device, or a handheld console (PSP, Nintendo DS, etc). You will also need one.

Play

- Write the following on the board and elicit the missing question words. Drill the questions.

  _____ is the name of the game? (What)
  _____ do you play it? (How)
  _____ do you have to do? (What)
  _____ lives do you have? (How many)
  _____ did it cost? (How much)
  _____ have you had this game? (How long)
  _____ do you like it? (Why)

- Take out your handheld device, turn it on and find a game. Show the whole class from a distance. Encourage them to ask you questions, using the question words as prompts. Answer the questions.

- Put the learners into pairs, A and B. Ask all the A students to take out their handheld devices and to switch them on. Tell them to find a game.
  - Student A now shows Student B the game and answers the questions on the board.
  - Once Student A has finished, Student B does the same.

- Monitor, and write any useful language on the board as it comes up. If a pair finishes, tell them to change partners. Repeat this a few times.

Play on

You can ask the learners to write a short 'magazine type' article about the game they chose.

Chapter Three
The connected classroom

A classroom that is centred round
a single connection does not have to mean
a teacher-centred classroom.

Engage your learners with digital games
in activities that will place the focus clearly
on *them* and *their* interests.

Those were the days

Things aren't what they used to be

○

The aim of the game
To watch an old computer game and discuss
how things have changed – for the better

Ⓛ Ⓢ ⓡ ⓦ

Prepare to play

Find a few videos (on YouTube or a similar site) of old computer games (*Pong*, *Donkey Kong*, etc). Ideally, they are games you once played yourself.

Play

● Ask the learners to talk in pairs about the following questions:
  - *What were the first computer games like?*
  - *How have things changed since then?*
  - *What aspects of computer games have changed? (graphics, music, story, etc)*
  - *How are games better now?*

● Tell the learners they are going to watch a few short videos showing old computer games. Write the titles of the games on the board.

● Ask if any of the names are familiar, and if any of the learners say yes, invite them to tell the rest of the class what they know about the games.

● Play the videos and say a few words about each game (what is happening in the video, the objective of the game, where it was played, etc).

● Ask the learners to talk together again in pairs about what things have changed, how games are better.

● Stop them after five minutes or so and open the discussion up to the whole class.

● When you have finished, you can tell the class about *your* experience playing the computer games in the videos.

Play on

You can tell the learners that they will probably find online the games in the videos you were watching: you can ask them to look for one of them, to play it and tell everyone what they think of it in the next class.

I spy in the game

Can you identify what you see?

○

The aim of the game
To play *I Spy* with a puzzle game
to increase vocabulary

Ⓛ Ⓢ ⓡ ⓦ

Prepare to play

Use a 'hidden objects' game that has objects relevant to the level and interests of your class. Have a class set of dictionaries to hand.

Play

● Display the first game screen and tell the learners to look up and write down the words in English for all of the objects that they have to identify in the game.

● Next, play the game and ask the learners to tell you where the hidden objects are (eg *The glass of orange is on the table next to the vase*).

● When they describe something well, follow the learners' instructions to play the game. If there are difficulties, reformulate the language and write it on the board as you do so.

● If you like, you can ask the learner who correctly formulates a sentence to come to the board and play the next part of the game.

● Play until the end of the first screen of the game. If the timer runs out, repeat the first level and ask the learners to repeat their descriptions of where the objects are.

● If the learners like it, play another couple of levels.

Play on

You can ask the learners to play the next level of the game at home and to write a description of where the objects are.

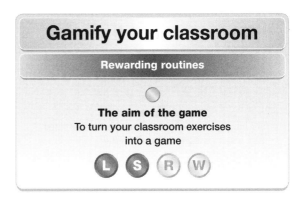

Prepare to play

Choose a 'casual' game such as *Farmville* or a 'simulation' game based on a topic you are studying in class. This activity works better if you use a game that you know some of your learners have played.

Play

- Open the game in class and ask your learners if they know it. If some of them do, ask them to tell the others briefly what the objective is and how the game is played. If nobody knows the game, the learners make predictions.

- Start playing the game and deliberately make mistakes. Ask the learners to tell you what to do, instructing you each step of the way. Help them express themselves as you play, and make a record of any useful language on the board as you go along.

- Finish playing once you say you have got the hang of playing the game and ask the learners to write down a list of things that someone who doesn't know the game needs to understand in order to play.

- Monitor the learners while they are writing and help with any difficult language.

- When they have finished, ask them to compare their instructions and revise as appropriate.

- Finish with a discussion about the game as opposed to farming in the *real* world:
  - *What differences are there?*
  - *What similarities?*

Play on

The learners can exchange instructions with a partner and check them at home by playing the game.

Prepare to play

Use one of the 'incentive' games such as *www.chorewars.com* or *www.plusoneme.com* and set up an account. If you use *Chore Wars*, you can set up accounts for each learner; if it is *Plus One Me*, you'll need your learners' emails to be able to send them a 'gold star' when they accomplish something.

Play

- Introduce the learners to the site and explain that you are going to use it to reward them for all the hard work they do in class.
  - If you decide to use *Plus One Me*, share everyone's emails and tell the learners that they, too, can award gold stars to their classmates if they think someone deserves it.
  - With *Chore Wars*, work together to turn the exercises, tests and exams that you usually do into adventures. How to do this will be apparent when you go to the site, but what you will need to do together is to decide how many 'experience points' each test, exam, etc, is worth. This can lead to a reflective discussion about what things the learners find more difficult.

- Log into the site each time you have a class with the learners and keep a record of the good work they do by awarding points when they deserve them.

Play on

You can ask the learners to create their own accounts and use the sites to record and reward what they and the others do for homework.

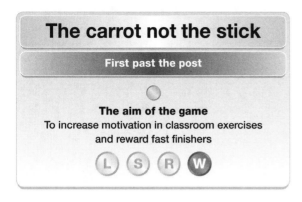

The carrot not the stick

First past the post

The aim of the game
To increase motivation in classroom exercises
and reward fast finishers

L S R **W**

Prepare to play

Use an 'incentive' game such as *Flight* (*armorgames.com/
play/7598/flight*) for this. The games that work best are those
that can be played and completed in a very short space of
time.

Play

- This game is effectively played as a motivation to learners
  for completing exercises (gap fills, comprehension checks,
  etc) from coursebooks.

- Use the game as a reward and by telling the learners that
  the first person to complete the exercise correctly can
  have a turn playing the game.

- As soon as the first learner has completed the task, stop
  the others and ask that learner to read out what they
  think is the correct answer. If it's correct, then ask the
  learner to come up to the computer and play the game.

- To make sure a different learner wins the next time, you
  can set the next task while the winner is still standing at
  the computer – to give the others a head start.

- Keep playing until there are no exercises left.

Play on

You can ask the learners to identify another similar game
they would like to use as the incentive next time you do this.

Shooting the breeze

Talking and gaming

The aim of the game
To use a game as a fun incentive
for fluency practice

L **S** R W

Prepare to play

Choose a 'first person shooter' game that clearly gives points
to the player. Also prepare notes to talk about a particular
subject you want the class to speak about.

Play

- Demonstrate the activity by giving a short talk yourself
  while a volunteer learner plays the game.

- Tell the learners that they are going to be working in pairs
  as a team, playing a computer game for points and giving
  a talk to the rest of the class.
    - They are going to prepare a one-minute talk
      about a particular subject (this can be about
      anything – *hobbies*, *daily routines*, etc).
    - They will have to speak for a minute or more.

- Give them five minutes to write notes for their talk.

- While one of them talks with their back to the screen, the
  other plays the game. If the talker pauses for more than
  five seconds the screen will be turned off and the game
  and the talk ends.

- One learner sits at the game and the other has their back to
  the board. The gamer starts as soon as the speaker begins.

- Start the activity. Stand by the screen with a stopwatch.

- If there is a pause, count down by raising your hand and
  counting down the seconds on your hand. If you reach
  five, switch the screen off and stop the pair.

- As soon as you've switched the screen off ask the player to
  sit down. Switch the screen back on and make a note of
  their score on the board.

- Continue with the next pairs in the class and finally add
  up the scores and declare the winning team.

Play on

The learners can prepare a talk at home and practise playing
the game so they get a better score next time.

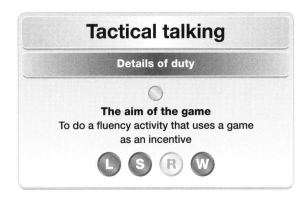

Tactical talking

Details of duty

The aim of the game
To do a fluency activity that uses a game as an incentive

L S (R) (W)

Prepare to play

For this activity, you'll need a 'first person shooter' game with a lot of movement. Play the game and think about whether the language needed to give instructions to the character is appropriate to the level of your class.

Play

- Ask the learners if they know what a mercenary is (*a soldier who fights for money*). Tell them that they have hired a mercenary who is very happy to fight for them but will only do exactly what they tell them to do.

- Put learners into teams and ask them to observe carefully as you play a game.

- Stop after a minute and turn the screen of the game off. Tell each team that they are to write instructions to the mercenary, based on what needs to be done in the game.

- Set a time limit of five minutes and help the teams with any language they need, but don't help them remember what happens in the game.

- When the time is up, collect the written instructions and ask a volunteer learner to start to play the game as you read. Tell this learner that they must do exactly what you say and not react 'normally' in the game.

- The learner plays the game, following the spoken instructions until they lose a life. At this point, make a note of the score, change the volunteer and read a different team's text.

- Continue until all of the teams' texts have been read.

- When all the texts have been read out, give them back and ask the teams to rewrite them to make them better.

- If there's time and interest, play another round, count up the score and declare the winning team.

Play on

You can introduce the learners to a different game and ask them to play it and write a set of instructions for homework.

Little monster

Classroom pet

The aim of the game
To make looking after a virtual pet a regular part of your class

L S (R) (W)

Prepare to play

This activity is designed for young learner classes and you'll need to select a 'virtual pet' game such as *Moshi Monsters* (*www.moshimonsters.com*).

Play

- Set up an account with the site (if appropriate) and think about whether you want to share the user name and password with the class. The advantage of this is that the members of the class can 'look after' the virtual pet in between classes.

- Introduce the site to the learners and decide on a name for the virtual pet. If there are any other choices to be made, work through these together and negotiate, taking a vote if it's not clear what a decision should be.

- We suggest you do not play for longer than 10–15 minutes each class. It also works best if you have a specific regular timeslot in your lessons when you play with this pet (ie at the beginning, or just after a break).

- Be sure to make the most out of the virtual pet by talking to the learners while you play, deciding together on what to do next.

Play on

The virtual pet will also serve as a character in stories that you then ask the learners to write.

We can walk it out

Reconstruction work

The aim of the game
To work together to reconstruct a walkthrough
while playing the game

(L) (S) (R) (W)

Prepare to play

Find the walkthrough of an 'adventure game' and remove some of the key nouns from the beginning section (as in the example opposite). Print off copies for all the learners. Get the game ready to play on a screen at the front of the class.

Play

● Show the learners the introduction to the game. Help them with any language that they don't understand, to make sure they know both the story and its objective.

● At the first screen, brainstorm as many vocabulary items as you can in five minutes. Write the words on the board and explain the meaning of difficult vocabulary.

● In pairs, tell the learners to use the words on the board to tell their partner how they think you play the game. Monitor and input language as necessary.

● Give out a copy of the walkthrough and ask a volunteer to start playing the game. Tell the learners who aren't playing to use the guide to give instructions to the player, suggesting nouns based on what they can see on the screen.

● Encourage the learners to put their hand up if they have an idea, and write any new language that they produce on the board. Encourage them not to repeat verbs (particularly 'click'). Any useful language should be copied down later in their notebooks.

● Change the learner playing the game from time to time and continue playing until you reach the end of the first part of the game.

● Stop the activity and tell the learners to listen as you read the original walkthrough. As you read, ask them to check the words they suggested.

Play on

The learners can play the next part of the game at home and write instructions, looking up the nouns and verbs that are unfamiliar. Check their walkthroughs during the next class.

The Stone Circle – Arcane Season (Part 2)

1 Go down the _____ .

2 Click on the man and then his _____ .

3 Click on the _____ and drag it to the water in front of the bar gate.

4 Now use your infra-red binoculars. You will see a small _____ glowing.

5 Look just to the left where you are standing and click on the _____ .

6 On the machine, push the following buttons in order: 4, 6, 2, 5 (from left to right).

7 Click on the upper right corner to exit and then open the glowing _____ .

8 Pick up the three objects – the _____ , the hand of the beast and the dream-catcher.

9 Go back to the machine with buttons and pull the _____ .

10 To exit from the warehouse door click on the following buttons in this exact order: 3, 2, 1, 2, 4, 2, 5.

11 Below the warehouse stairs is a _____ . Click on it to get the crowbar.

12 Now click on the warehouse door upstairs.

13 Go back downstairs where you found that man.

14 Use the bar above the gate to go to the other side.

The beginning of
http://www.gamershood.com/flashgames/137

Answers

1 stairs	4 box	8 note
2 bottle	5 wrench	9 lever
3 pallet	7 box	11 tool box

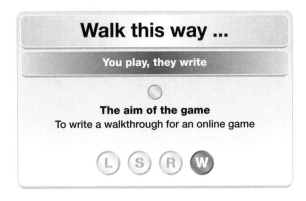

Walk this way ...

You play, they write

The aim of the game
To write a walkthrough for an online game

L S R **W**

Play/write

Play together, write together

The aim of the game
To play a computer game
and write the story as a team

L **S** R **W**

Prepare to play

Find a short 'point and click' game and print off a copy of the walkthrough for yourself.

Play

- Display the 'point and click' game on the board. Ask the learners what they can see. Elicit a couple of answers.

- Tell the learners you are going to play the game. They must write down the things you click on. Do an example first, and check the answer.

- As you play the game, using the walkthrough, allow time for the learners to write a list of object names. (They should leave room on the left – to write the verbs later.)

- When the game – or the first level of the game, if it is long – is finished, ask for feedback, to make sure everyone has a complete set of the objects in the game.

- In pairs, the learners take it in turn to tell each other how to complete the game, using the list of objects.

- Tell the learners they are going to watch the game played again and, this time, they have to write a verb in front of each object in their list. However, they should extend their range of action verbs: they cannot use the word 'click' and they aren't allowed to repeat verbs.

- At this point, you could invite a learner to come and play. Play the game as before and, when it is finished, the learners compare their notes and discuss any differences.

- Finally, the learners write out the walkthrough, using complete sentences – with the verbs and objects they wrote down, and adding any details they can.

Play on

The learners can be given links to two or three other 'point and click' games. They play one at home and write a walkthrough. They exchange them with a partner in the next class, to see if they can complete the game later, using the clues.

Prepare to play

Find a game that has a good narrative storyline with short video sequences, and play it using a walkthrough. As you play, think about possible language difficulties the learners may have. This activity works best if the learners have already practised narrative tenses – you might want to pre-teach some language items.

Play

- Explain to the learners that they are going to write the story of a computer game together – as they play it.

- Put them into groups of at least three or four learners.

- Invite one of the learners to start playing the game. Tell the others to observe everything that happens and to write notes about the story.

- Stop the gameplay after a few minutes and allow time for the learners to briefly discuss the story using their notes. One of them writes down the basic story.

- Ask for another volunteer, and continue the game. Give the volunteer help if necessary, using the walkthrough.

- Repeat this procedure until the story (and the game) comes to a conclusion.

- Next, tell the teams they are going to take the basic story they have written together and improve it.

- Monitor during this 'discussing and writing' stage, helping the learners with difficult language and encouraging them to use different narrative tenses, sequencers, adverbs and adjectives, etc.

- Finally, collect the teams' stories and make a class storybook.

Play on

You can give the learners copies of the storybook and ask them to take the best elements from several stories and write a new story for homework.

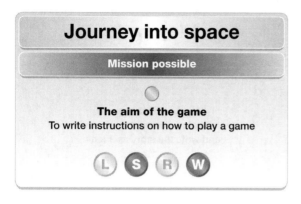

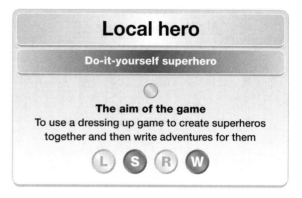

Journey into space

Mission possible

The aim of the game
To write instructions on how to play a game

Local hero

Do-it-yourself superhero

The aim of the game
To use a dressing up game to create superheros together and then write adventures for them

Prepare to play

Choose an 'arcade' game set in space, such as *Into Space* (*http://www.notdoppler.com/intospace.php*).

Prepare to play

Choose a suitable dressing up game that allows you to create superheroes, such as *Hero Machine*. Make sure you know how it works (*http://www.heromachine.com*).

Play

- Introduce the game to the class, playing it briefly and talking about the game's objective.

- Tell the learners they are going to be writing instructions and advice for the crew of the space ship featured in the game and ask them, in pairs or groups, to decide what information the crew will need on their mission. Give them an example or two (eg *Always wear your space suit. Don't fly too fast,* etc) to get them started and monitor while they are writing their sentences, helping with language as necessary.

- Next, invite one of the learners to start playing the game, and let this person play for a few minutes while the others pay careful attention. Stop the activity at a suitable point (when there's a break in the flow or a level is finished, etc).

- Ask the learners to look again at the instructions and advice they wrote and to change these, making additions based on what they have seen of the game.

- Choose a different learner to continue playing and stop again when appropriate. This time, after adding to the advice and instructions, ask the learners to guess what the crew needs to do in order to survive until the end of the mission.

Play

- Ask the learners to work in pairs, brainstorming a list of crimes and then decide together which ones are most frequent locally

- Write them as a 'Top Five' list on the board.

- Explain that you are going to create a superhero together to help combat these crimes, and ask the class to decide (before playing the game) on the powers the superhero would need, to be able to stop or prevent the crimes on the board. Write up the suggestions next to the crimes.

- Now go to the dressing up game and start creating the superhero together. Choose a look for the character and then capture the image and display it on the board.

- Together, decide on a suitable name for the superhero and write a description of the hero's identity and powers on the board – based on what you have decided so far (see the example below).

> *Julian is a musician by day but transforms into Jumper Julian the superhero at night. He is telepathic and monitors crime activity in his recording studio, collecting evidence to give to the police. His keyboard converts into a flying motorcycle and he parachutes into crime scenes. Bullets bounce off his protective suit and he extends his elastic arms to capture the criminals.*

Play on

You can ask the learners to continue playing at home and to prepare what they have written as a 'Crew training manual', with screenshots to illustrate what they have written.

Play on

The learners can choose one of the crimes and to write a newspaper article, describing what the criminals were doing and how they got caught by the superhero. Collect the stories and publish them as a class booklet.

Games frames

Still guessing

The aim of the game
To describe a game from a screenshot
and help other learners to guess it

L **S** R W

Prepare to play

Find some still images (screenshots) from famous games, using a search engine, and add them to your presentation software (PowerPoint or your IWB software, etc). At the bottom of each still, write a few words the learners must not use when describing the game (title, character names, etc).

Play

- One learner stands at the front of the class, their back to the board. Tell the rest of the learners they are going to describe a game to this learner – without using the words displayed at the bottom of the picture you are going to display.

- Display the still image, and the other learners help the person at the front to guess the game.

- When they do, another learner takes their place and you display a different image from a different game.

- After you finish, ask the learners to remember all of the games, and write them on the board. Discuss these questions:
  - *Which game was the hardest to guess? Why?*
  - *Which game was the easiest? Why?*
  - *Which words helped you guess the games?*

Play on

The learners can choose different games and write a short description (without mentioning the title, etc) that could be used to help someone guess the game. They then bring their texts to the next class and test each other.

Before and after

What's happened?

The aim of the game
To guess the changes that have taken place
in a game by comparing screenshots

L **S** R W

Prepare to play

Prepare 10–12 pairs of still images (screenshots) of games which show changes ('before and after' pictures) and create a slideshow presentation of the images.

You can either do this by playing the games yourself, which will take a lot of preparation as you will need to play a number of games and take screenshots of them, or you can find images that have already been taken by gamers. Alternatively, you can find videos of games (on YouTube, for example) and take the screenshots while watching.

Choose images that show clearly that something has changed from one image to the other. Put the screenshots together, using slideshow presentation software (PowerPoint, etc). Make sure you do this before the lesson!

Play

- Explain to the learners that they are going to see a sequence of two similar screenshots from games that show changes, and they are to guess what has happened to cause the change.

- Show the two images quickly at first and ask the learners for suggestions as to what has changed:
  - *The door has opened.*
  - *The light has been turned on.*

- Continue until the learners have guessed all the changes shown in all the pictures. Revise and correct the language as necessary.

Play on

You can play 'After and before' – with the learners *predicting* the changes, after they have seen the *first* image.

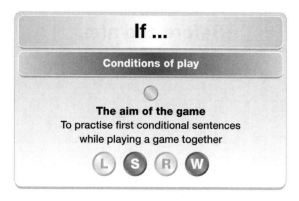

If ...

Conditions of play

The aim of the game
To practise first conditional sentences
while playing a game together

(L) (S) (R) (W)

Prepare to play

Find a 'point and click' or 'escape the room' game that has a strong story and find the walkthrough to go with it. Play part of the game yourself, using the walkthrough, to get a feel for the narrative, and write a sentence that acts as an introduction to the game story. See the example below.

> ***Samorost 2***
>
> You are living with your dog on a peaceful planet far far away, but one day a group of aliens decide to pay you a visit while you are sleeping.
>
> *http://amanita-design.net/samorost-2*

Play

- Display the game and briefly explain the background to the game's story to the learners, reading your introductory sentence.

- Ask the learners a question based on what you see at the beginning of the game. For instance (if using *Samorost 2*):
  - *What do you think will happen if I knock on the kennel?*

- Tell the learners they are to make predictions on what will happen if you perform a certain action, using a first conditional sentence. This works best if you have previously presented this tense with the class.

- Perform the first action, and give the learners the answer:
  - *If you knock on the dog's kennel, he will come out and bark at the aliens.*

- Ask the learners another question:
  - *What will happen if I knock on the window of the castle?*

- Encourage them to volunteer predictions:
  - *The owner will come out and look for his dog.*

- Continue until the first level of the game has been completed, or for 10–15 minutes, then stop and tell the learners you are going to test their memory. Write the first sentence on the board:
  - *If you knock on the dog's kennel, he will come out and bark at the aliens.*

- Ask the learners to remember the subsequent actions, encouraging them to form first conditional sentences, writing them on the board.

- Start playing the game again. This time, when you stop, ask the learners to write the conditional sentences in their notebooks. Monitor and check as they do so.

- Continue playing until the end of the game. If the game is long, stop after a few levels.

Play on

You can ask the learners to continue playing the game (or another similar one) at home and to write more example conditional sentences.

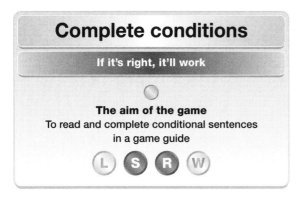

Complete conditions

If it's right, it'll work

The aim of the game
To read and complete conditional sentences
in a game guide

Prepare to play

Find a short 'point and click' game with a walkthrough. Prepare the first part of the walkthrough and change the first few lines into conditional sentences, as in the example opposite taken from the game *Quest for the Rest*. After printing a copy for yourself, remove the second part of the sentences and make a copy for each learner in the class.

Play

- Present the game and go through the introduction. Make sure the learners understand the story and what to do.

- After the introduction, elicit from the learners what they think you should do. Encourage the use of the first conditional, writing the first few suggestions on the board if necessary.

- Ask a volunteer to play the game, and hand out copies of the walkthrough to the other learners. They complete the conditional sentences as the game is being played.

- Change the volunteer player after every couple of sentences. As the game is played, ask the learners for their ideas and correct their language when necessary.

- If anyone uses the word 'click', tell them this is fine – but can they think of an alternative verb? If a verb is repeated, try to elicit another appropriate verb. This may prove difficult, but it can be very rewarding.

- For the second level of the game, ask the learners to write complete conditional sentences as they discover how the game works. Share these with the class, writing them on the board. If they are having difficulty progressing, read out from the walkthrough to help them.

- Play until the end of the game, or stop after a few levels.

Play on

For homework, the learners can play the next level of the game (or a different game) and write their own walkthrough, using conditional sentences.

Quest for the Rest

1 If you click on the cactus bumps, they will …

2 If one drops to the ground …

3 If three drop at the same time …

4 If you open the turtle's eyes …

5 If you wake the third person …

6 If the balloon is inflated …

http://www.questfortherest.com

Suggested answers
1 turn into fruit
2 a rat will come out of the cactus
3 they won't be eaten
4 it'll move to the fruit and eat it
5 she will blow up the balloon
6 the people will fly off to the second level

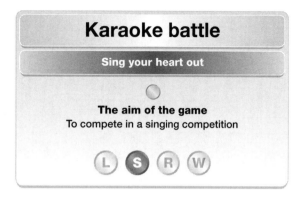

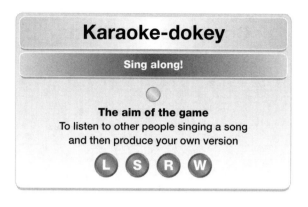

Prepare to play

If you have access to a console and a game such as *SingStar*, then use this. If not, find an online karaoke site that lets two or more players compete – such as *www.karaokeparty.com*. You will have to sign up for an account beforehand. Make sure you have a microphone and speakers attached to the computer you are going to use.

Play

- Check that at least some of your learners are happy about singing in English in front of the class – if there are no takers, don't force them to do it.

- Open the game and choose the competitive mode (it's called 'battle' at the *Karaoke Party* site) and ask for a group of learners to volunteer for a *karaoke battle* (ie to see who can sing the song best).
  - If you're using *SingStar*, your learners will be competing against themselves.
  - If using *Karaoke Party*, then choose 'public battle' mode and either select a song that others have chosen, or initiate a new song.

- While you're waiting for the battle to start, you can chat to the other players: suggest to one of the learners that they introduce the group.

- Once the battle begins, the score depends on how well the group are able to sing the song – points will also be displayed.

- Once the song has finished, make a note of the points and deal with issues of pronunciation. Then invite the next group to choose a song or join in an existing karaoke battle.

Play on

You can persuade any learners who are interested in doing so to sign up for their own account on the karaoke website – and go on singing.

Prepare to play

Sign up for an account on a karaoke website that lets you listen to other people's songs. You can use one such as *http://www.singsnap.com/karaoke*. Make sure you have working speakers and microphone on the computer in the classroom.

Play

- Ask the learners to suggest songs in English they think they could sing, and write a number of them up on the board.

- Log in to the karaoke site and search for the first song. If you don't find it, look for the next one – until you find a song the learners have chosen that has already been sung by others on the site.

- Listen to and watch (some of the songs have videos) the version of the song, and read the comments that have been posted below it. Deal with any vocabulary that may be unfamiliar and, together, prepare and leave a (positive) comment on the recording.

- Listen to another version of the song and read the comments. Write a comment on this recording, too.

- Next, ask for volunteers to sing a class version of the song. When you've finished, check the comments to see if anyone has written any.

- Choose another song and repeat the process.

Play on

If your learners enjoy this, why not make it a once-monthly class activity? And don't forget to check the comments to see what people write.

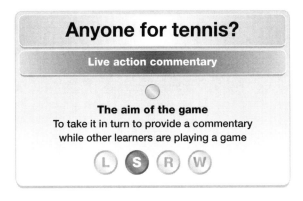

Anyone for tennis?

Live action commentary

The aim of the game
To take it in turn to provide a commentary
while other learners are playing a game

Prepare to play

The popular *Nintendo Wii Sports* is good for this, as it
includes a number of different sports (tennis, golf, ten-pin
bowling, etc) and the games are short. However, not to
worry if you don't have access to a *Wii* – any sports game
will do.

If you do have a *Wii*, before the learners arrive set up the
game console in the classroom and select one of the sports
(tennis is our example, as it works particularly well).

Play

- Display the game on the screen and ask the learners what
  they know about it, eliciting the related vocabulary.

- Write the vocabulary the learners suggest, and any other
  necessary words, on the board so they can all see.

- Elicit what a sports commentator does. Ask the learners
  to work in pairs and come up with some typical
  expressions a tennis commentator would say (see the
  examples below).

  Love all
  30-love
  Deuce
  Advantage Nadal
  Federer to serve
  Good serve
  Great shot!
  What a wonderful volley
  Match point
  Game, set and match

- Review their phrases and write the best examples on the
  board, adding your own examples, too.

- Recruit two volunteers to play a short tennis match, and
  tell the other learners they are going to take turns to be
  the commentator.

- The two players start, but pause between serves to give
  the others enough time to be able to commentate.

- Ask a volunteer to begin commentating.

- Continue playing and change the commentator from
  time to time.

- At the end of the game, ask the volunteer commentators
  what they thought was most difficult about their job.

- Ask the class:
  - Did having the typical phrases written on the
    board help?
  - Was there anything they needed to say that wasn't
    on the board?
  - Did they want to add these to the board?

- Choose another two volunteers, and play another game
  or two until everyone has had a turn commentating.

Play on

A good follow-up activity would be a discussion about the
differences in commentating between different sports.

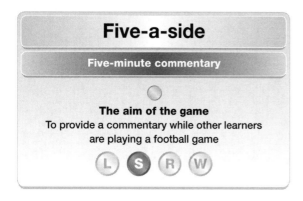

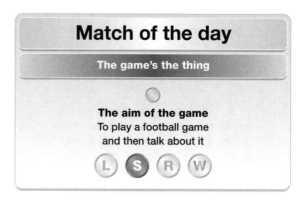

Prepare to play

Any football game on a game console would be ideal for this. Alternatively, there are online football games you can play.

Play

◉ Display the football game on the screen and ask the learners to talk about TV and radio commentators:
  • Why are commentators used?
  • What does a good commentary add to a match?

◉ Brainstorm together some typical phrases a football commentator would say and write them on the board.

◉ Add some more examples, as appropriate, to what's on the board and stop when you have a reasonable selection.

◉ Next, divide the class into several groups of five.

◉ Choose one of the groups, ask for two volunteers to play the football match and tell the other three learners they are going to be a panel of commentators. Tell them they can talk together about how well the players are doing, who they think will score the next goal, etc. Most importantly, there shouldn't be any long pauses or you'll stop the game and ask another group to play. Tell them their objective is to commentate for five minutes.

◉ Continue playing, changing groups when their five minutes are up or if they pause for too long.

◉ While the learners are speaking, take note of what they say, and write some example sentences with errors in them for use in an eventual penalty shoot-out.

◉ When all the groups have played, declare the winner – the group that managed to speak for five minutes.

◉ If more than one group did, hold a penalty shoot-out quizzing them on the mistakes in their sentences.

Play on

If this activity is successful, you can play it again with other sports games, such as car driving games, etc.

Prepare to play

Choose a football game or, even better, use a football game on any of the popular games consoles (if you have access to one).

Play

◉ Divide the class into two football teams and ask each team to choose a name and decide who is the team manager. The manager then chooses three or four tactical advisors. The rest of the team are the players.

◉ The management team decides on the order the players are to play.

◉ Start the football game, with one player in each team going head to head for one minute. Change the players every minute and let the game continue for five minutes before calling half-time.

◉ If you want to, and can, provide a running commentary while the game is being played.

◉ At half-time, the managers have to prepare advice for the teams and decide on the new player order, to be given in writing to the referee (the teacher).

◉ The second half begins. The game is played in the same way as the first half. After five minutes, blow the final whistle and declare a winning team.

◉ If the score is a draw, the match goes to *penalties* – ask both teams a question about football – the team that answers the most questions correctly wins.

◉ At the end of the game, the teacher acts as TV reporter, interviewing the managers and different players about the match.

Play on

Ask the learners to write a match report. They can also watch a couple of videos of football players and managers talking in English after a game.

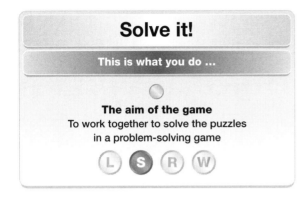

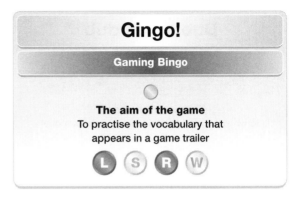

Prepare to play

Choose a suitable puzzle game such as *Crayon Physics Deluxe* (*http://www.crayonphysics.com*) that requires simple instructions to complete and find the video walkthrough on YouTube.

Play

- Start the game, and demonstrate how it works by talking the learners through the first couple of introductory screens – explaining the objective and the concepts behind the game.

- When they have got the idea, ask for a few volunteers to tell you how to proceed (how you can move the ball so that it touches the star in our example game).

- Listen to their ideas and ask them to choose the one they think will work best. Ask that learner to come out and test their solution to see if it works.

- Continue in this way (it will probably get more difficult as it goes on) and, each time, ask the learners to explain exactly what they plan to do, before letting them try to do it. Deal with any new vocabulary as it emerges, and keep a record of it on the board or a piece of paper (to review later).

- Finally, show the learners the video walkthrough, and ask them to compare the differences between how *they* solved the problems and how the person in the video solved them.

Play on

You can ask the learners to play another similar game and write instructions to the first few screens – in other words, to write a walkthrough themselves.

Prepare to play

Find a game trailer on YouTube or a similar site. Watch it, and prepare a list of words or phrases that occur. Add some words that aren't in the trailer. The example below uses the official trailer for *The Sims 3*, where the words are written, so the activity is a reading activity.

The Sims 3

insane	sane	clumsy	careful	party animal
hard-working	disobey	obey	share	keep
hate	love	outdoors	indoors	online	offline
life	death	rock star	accountant	astronaut
	master criminal	police officer	miner	

Play

- Write your list of words up on the board. As you do so, check that the learners know them. Teach the meaning of any they don't know and practise the pronunciation.

- Hand out a 3 x 3 Bingo card, or ask the learners to draw one. Ask them to choose nine words from the board and copy them into the spaces.

- Tell the learners they are going to watch a trailer for a video game and play a gaming version of Bingo. As they watch the trailer, they should cross out on their card each word they see or hear. The first person to cross out all their words shouts *Gingo!*

- After playing the trailer, if nobody wins, ask the learners to change their words – and play the game again.

Play on

Ask the learners to find another game trailer and to prepare a *Gingo!* activity of their own for the next class.

Dub a dub dub

Voicing a game video

The aim of the game
To write the dialogue to a clip of a promotional video and put voices to it

(L) (S) (R) (W)

Prepare to play

Choose a short promo video for a game (from YouTube or a similar video sharing site) that the class will be familiar with and like. Find or transcribe the dialogue of the scene, and produce a handout with words missing, making enough copies for all the learners (as in the example opposite).

Play

- Ask the learners if they have played the game you have chosen and, if so, get them to tell you what it is about.
- Tell them they are going to work in pairs or small groups and watch a video promoting the game – but without being able to hear what is said.
- Tell them to take notes while they watch and try to guess the actual words that are being said.
- Play the video several times, pausing as necessary.
- When you are ready, ask the learners to take turns and say their words in real time, dubbing the video as it plays.
- Hold a vote for the best/funniest/silliest/most serious version, etc.
- Next, hand out the transcript and play the video again, this time with sound. Ask the learners to add the missing words.
- Finally, they compare the actual words to what *they* came up with. How close were they?

Play on

For homework, the learners find a promo video to another game and prepare it for the next class – they can either make up the dialogue or use the actual words that are said in the film. Hold a film festival and give awards for the best script/ voice actor, etc.

L A Noire

- We'll get a commendation if we 1) _____ this murder code.
- Are you 2) _____ that the homicide squad won't step in and take the collar?
- Even if they do, we 3) _____ along and who knows we might get bumped up a desk.
- That's him! 4) _____ him!
- Hey, whadda you … Someone 5) _____ that guy!
- This guy thinks he's at the 6) _____ .
- Nothing to see here. Let's 7) _____ along.

Answers
1 crack
2 sure
3 play
4 get
5 stop
6 speedway
7 move

Teaser trailer

A game promo video

The aim of the game
To plan and write a short promotional video
advertising a game

Freeze!

Don't any of you move …

The aim of the game
To create *tableaux vivants* of a game
as you play it

Teaser trailer

Prepare to play

Using YouTube, find an example teaser trailer for a game the learners will know. Write a short description of the trailer (see the example below) and make a copy for each learner.

> *The trailer begins by showing us an image of the hero of the game. The music is dramatic and you can hear strange birds in the distance. There is a close-up of the hero's face and the title of the game is displayed. A voice tells us what to expect and …*

Play

- Show the learners the trailer. Then ask them to work in pairs and discuss the game advertised. How does it attract the viewer's attention? Use question prompts:
  - *What effects do they use?*
  - *Is there a voiceover?*
  - *What about the language?*
  - *What about the music?*
- Tell the learners they are going to prepare a teaser trailer of a game with a partner. Ask them to find someone who knows a game they both know well, and to brainstorm ideas for the trailer together.
- Give the learners the copy of your text explaining the trailer and, after they have read it, watch the trailer again.
- Tell them they are going to work with their partner and write a similar text for another game they both know.
- Once the scripts have been written, ask the learners to read them out to the class. If you like, you can also make a voice recording of them reading from their texts.

Play on

The learners can find the actual teaser trailer of the game they chose and practise reading their text at home with the sound turned down, ready to read it aloud next class while the trailer is playing.

Freeze!

Prepare to play

Choose a game with lots of things happening – and with at least three or four people involved in the action. You will also need to clear a space in the room.

Play

- Divide the learners into groups of three or four and show them the game you are going to use.
- Start playing.
- Tell one of the learners in the class to shout out the word *Freeze!* whenever they want to. When they do, all the groups have to physically arrange themselves so as to reproduce what is on the screen.
- Continue playing the game but, this time, make sure the other learners cannot see what's happening on the screen (by turning off the projector and/or moving the computer screen so they can't see it).
- Choose another volunteer and ask them to shout out *Freeze!* after a short period of time.
- This time, the learner who shouted '*Freeze!*' has to describe the scene in the game to the others, who have to reproduce it physically in their groups.
- Take note of any language that causes difficulty.
- Continue a few more times, and then show the game again. Finish by writing up on the board examples of language that the learners had trouble with and practising ways to improve it.

Play on

You can ask the learners to look for a different game that could be used, instead of the one you chose. They can do this at home then, in the next class, they describe their games and the learners take a vote on which one to use for a repeat of the activity.

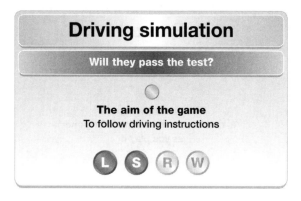

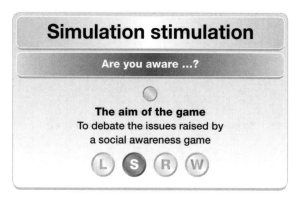

Prepare to play

Find a driving game that can be used for this activity. A good one is *http://geoquake.jp/en/webgame/DrivingSimulator*. Note that you won't be able to do all of the actions described below if you use other games.

Play

- Tell the learners they have a test. Then tell them it's not what they think – it's a driving test!

- Elicit/teach these verbs and write them on the board:
    brake
    accelerate
    turn right/left
    go forward
    go backwards (reverse)
    overtake
    slow down

- Show the learners the game, explain the controls (ie which keys to press for each of the verbs) and write the keyboard letter/symbol next to the verbs on the board, for reference.

- Ask for the first volunteer driver and tell them they are to do exactly as you say.

- Start giving instructions and watch how the learner performs. If they make a mistake, ask them to go back to their seat and invite another volunteer to 'take the wheel'.

- Continue playing, with learners taking turns driving and you giving instructions.

- Finally, invite the learners one by one to be the instructor and continue until all of them have played the game.

Play on

If they enjoy this activity, you can play a variation – using a flight simulator – with different language

Prepare to play

Choose one of the simulation games that relate to a strong social issue such as *Third World Farmer*, and play part of the game yourself to get a better idea of the issues and possible discussion themes that may arise.

Play

- When the game is set up, briefly explain what has to be done in order to play.

- Once the learners understand how the game is played, ask them to form groups and to decide on the first course of action. Set a time limit for group discussion and monitor the learners, helping them with language where needed.

- Listen to each group present their ideas of what they think should be done, and then take a vote on the course of action.

- Continue the game, making decisions based on popular vote, until you reach a natural pause in the game.

- Stop the game and ask the learners to talk about it so far:
    • What actions have been taken?
    • Were they the correct courses of action to take?
    • Were there mistakes to be learned from?

- Encourage the learners to say what went wrong and how they would do things differently the next time.

- Depending on the game, open the discussion up and get ideas about what it must really be like for people in this situation (third world farmers, people under threat of a natural disaster, etc).

Play on

A good follow-up activity would be to ask the learners to write a report on what they have learnt from the game and the discussion.

Chapter Four
Multiple connections

Whichever way you connect,
you can use the game plans in this chapter
to get your learners to learn while actively using
computer games in your lessons.

Use these activities – and appeal to the
learning styles and interests of the
21st century learner.

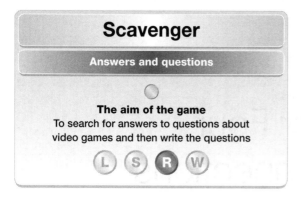

Scavenger

Answers and questions

The aim of the game
To search for answers to questions about video games and then write the questions

(L) (S) (R) (W)

Prepare to play

Prepare a number of questions for the learners to answer, or use the examples opposite.

Play

● Tell the learners they are to work in teams of two or three to take part in an internet 'scavenger hunt' and they will have to use search engines to find the answers. The first team to find the right answer to a question wins a point.

● **Round One**
Read out the first question and tell the learners to look for the answer. Continue until the end of your list of questions and then declare the pair with the most points the winners of the first round.

● **Round Two**
Next, ask the learners to recreate the questions you asked, giving a point to the first team who writes the first question exactly as you formulated it. Continue for each of the five questions, awarding points.

● **Round Three**
Tell each team to write their own question about computer games and to find the answer. They then take it in turn to ask the others to hunt for the answer to their question. Award points for this, the third round of the game.

● Add up the points and declare the winning team, then focus on any queries about question forms that may have occurred during Round Three.

Play on

For homework, you can ask the learners to prepare a set of five similar questions about another subject for others to answer. Re-distribute them the next class and set these questions as the next homework.

Scavenger hunt

1 *What was the best-selling PC game of all time?*
2 *When was the first video game console made?*
3 *What sport did the game Pong simulate?*
4 *Who created the game character Mario?*
5 *What was the first 3D video game called?*
6 *Where is Durotar?*
7 *What was the original name for Microsoft's Kinect?*
8 *What game is Alexey Pazhitnov famous for?*
9 *What is the Prince of Persia's real name?*
10 *How many characters are there in* Shadow of the Colossus?
11 *What was the first song from a video game to win a Grammy?*
12 *What animal is on a Nemean Cestus?*

Answers
1 *The Sims*
2 *1972 (Odyssey)*
3 *Table tennis*
4 *Shigeru Miyamot*
5 *Monster Maze*
6 *In Kalimdor (*World of Warcraft*)*
7 *Project Natal*
8 *Tetris*
9 *He doesn't have one.*
10 *19 (Wander, the horse, Mono, and 16 colossi)*
11 *Baba Yetu (from* Civilization IV*)*
12 *A lion (God of War)*

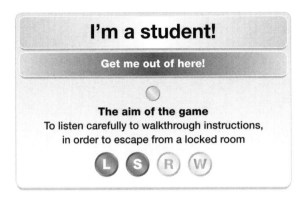

I'm a student!

Get me out of here!

The aim of the game
To listen carefully to walkthrough instructions,
in order to escape from a locked room

L S R W

Prepare to play

Find an 'escape the room' game and look for the guide, or use the example opposite (from the game *MOTAS*).

Play

- Sitting at their computers, ask the learners to work in pairs and open the game you have chosen.

- Tell the learners what the objective of the game is (to escape the room) and that, in order to do this, they have to do the following:
  - listen carefully
  - follow your instructions
  - ask questions when they don't understand

- Talk them through the game, using your walkthrough – or the solution opposite if you're playing *MOTAS*. Adapt your language to suit the level of your learners.

- Encourage the learners to respond to you as you move through the game, and ask them any follow-up questions that are appropriate.

- Check their understanding of the language, by observing their progress on-screen. Encourage discussion and negotiate the meaning of difficult vocabulary – asking them to provide definitions and ask other learners where necessary.

- Keep playing until the learners have escaped the first level.

Play on

The students can be given written instructions (from the walkthrough) for Levels 2 and 3 and you can ask them to use these to play at home. Ask them to tell you how it went next class.

Mystery of Time and Space (MOTAS)
Level one

You wake up and find yourself in a locked room. How can you escape?

Let's find things in the room to help you.

First, can you take anything from the wall? (yes, the poster)

Now, go to the bed and look under the pillow. What do you find? (a key)

Get the key and try to open the door. Can you? (no)

Go to the locker to the left of the room. Can you open this with the key? (yes)

Open the box in the bottom of the locker. What do you find? (a screwdriver)

Can you see anything to unscrew? (yes, the painting)

Now look at the lock of the door. What's in the keyhole? (the key)

How can you knock the key onto the other side of the door? (using the screw)

How can you catch the key when it falls from the lock? (using the poster)

OK, so first slide the poster under the door.

Then use the thin screw to push the key out of the lock.

Now, let's see, is the key to the door on the poster? (yes)

So, what are you waiting for?

Open the door – and escape the room!

http://www.albartus.com/motas/

On the run

Relay reading against the clock

The aim of the game
To take it in turn to read a game walkthrough and tell a partner how to finish part of a game

(L) (S) **R** (W)

That's not right

Correct as you play

The aim of the game
To correct a game guide that has incorrect information

(L) (S) **R** (W)

Prepare to play

Choose a short 'point and click' game and find the walkthrough. Start playing the game yourself and, while doing this, change the language in the walkthrough to suit the level of your learners. Print one copy to use as the relay text, and make a copy for each learner to look at afterwards.

Play

○ Tell the learners that they are going to have a race to see who can complete a game first. Show them the text and place it on a wall, away from the computers. Explain that they have to work in pairs and take turns to read and tell their partner what to do next.

○ In their pairs, they choose who starts playing the game and who reads the text.

○ Begin the activity and change roles after two or three minutes.

○ Play until one pair finishes the game or until time runs out.

○ Back in class formation, look at the text together and focus on the language. Deal with difficult vocabulary and discuss the game:
  - *Did you enjoy it?*
  - *What was the most difficult part?*

Play on

You can ask the learners to prepare and give a short presentation about their favourite digital game, comparing it with the game that you played in class and saying what it is about the game that they like so much.

Prepare to play

Find a 'point and click' game with a short walkthrough and edit it, changing some of the clues for the learners to correct. For example:
  - *Pick up the red key under the chair.* (It's a blue key.)
  - *Put the poster next to the door.* (Put it under the door.)
  - *Pick up the book under the pillow.* (There's a key under the pillow.)

Play

○ Hand out the walkthrough and tell the learners that they are going to play a game, find the mistakes in the walkthrough and correct them.

○ The learners look at the walkthrough and predict where some mistakes might be.

○ In pairs at their computers, one learner now plays the game while the other reads the walkthrough and corrects the mistakes.

○ They change places after a short time (eg five minutes).

○ Stop the activity when one pair finishes the game.

○ Discuss the answers, back in class formation.

Play on

The learners can choose a different game, find the walkthrough and prepare it in a similar way for a classmate.

Prepare to play

Choose a game and be prepared to direct the learners to it. Also have the walkthrough ready for Level One (you will be dictating the first two lines of this) and a copy of it for each learner, to give out at the end.

Play

- Put the learners into pairs.

- Direct them to the game and ask them to open a word processor too. Explain that they are going to play a game but they have to write the walkthrough as they play it.

- Tell them that the winning pair will be the one whose instructions most resemble the instructions you have.

- Make sure all the learners have a blank word processing document open on their screens. Dictate the first part of the walkthrough. When you've finished, tell the learners to use the dictation to start the game, and then to continue writing when they have 'played' the dictation.

- The learners play the game and write the instructions in the word processing document.

- Monitor, and if you see a pair playing but not writing, ask them to start the game from the beginning.

- Stop the activity when the first pair have finished.

- Hand out the walkthroughs and ask the learners to compare what they have written with these instructions. In particular, draw their attention to differences in vocabulary.

- Declare the winning team, and tell the learners to play and write the walkthrough of Level One of a different game for homework.

Play on

Next time you are working with computers, you can hand out the walkthroughs written as homework and ask the learners to play the game and make amendments if necessary.

Prepare to play

Find an online game which has a walkthrough on YouTube. It should be a game that is difficult to do without instructions (an 'escape the room' game, for example). This activity requires one computer per learner and is done in pairs – one learner is the gamer, the other watches the YouTube video and tells their partner how to play – so make sure that the gamer can't easily see the YouTube walkthrough.

Play

- Put the learners into pairs – Learner A is the *guide* and Learner B the *gamer*, each at their computers.
  - Learner A sits and watches the YouTube game video. They can pause or replay the video as many times as they want.
  - Meanwhile, Learner B gets familiar with the game.

- Learner A (the guide) relays how to play the game to the gamer (Learner B).

- After five minutes, the learners exchange seats.

- The first pair to finish the game, or to have got the furthest within a time limit (half an hour, for example), is the winner.

- Follow up with a discussion in class formation about how easy/difficult the game was and how easy/difficult it was to describe what was happening in the video.

Play on

The learners can prepare and give a short presentation about their favourite digital game, telling everyone what is difficult or what is easy about the game.

CHAPTER FOUR • MULTIPLE CONNECTIONS

Whisper walkthrough

Chain of instructions

The aim of the game
To send instructions down a line
to a learner playing a game

(L) (S) (R) (W)

Prepare to play

Choose a 'point and click' or 'escape the room' game that has a short walkthrough. Edit the instructions so that the language is appropriate for your learners' English level (see the example opposite) and print out copies.

As this is a team game, place three or four chairs (depending on the class size) in a line leading away from each team computer, with a printed copy of the walkthrough on the last chair. Set up the game on each computer – ready to play.

Play

○ Organise the learners into teams at the computers.

○ Tell them they are going to whisper the game instructions to each other. They will be penalised for cheating (you will take the instructions off them for five seconds). Cheating includes:
  • telling a teammate out of turn
  • using their mother tongue
  • moving out of their seat
However, stress that the learner with the walkthrough can stand up and look at the screen.

○ Begin the game:
  • The learner sitting on the last chair uses the printed copy of the walkthrough and whispers the first of the instructions to the person sitting next to them, and so on.
  • The learner sitting at the computer uses the information received to play the game.

○ After two or three minutes, the learner sitting at the front stands up, goes and sits at the back of the line, taking the walkthrough, while the others move one place forward.

○ The instructions get whispered down the line, in turn, until the learner at the computer is able to finish the game.

○ Back in class formation, ask the learners, in the same teams, to reconstruct the walkthrough text from memory. The team that comes closest to reproducing the walkthrough is then declared the winner.

The Blue Chamber

1 Go to the desk with the phone on it.
2 Open the drawer and take the pen.
3 Turn around and face the chair.
4 Click on the cushion and take the piece of paper.
5 Go to the pole thing on the wall and take the cylinder out of it.
6 Click on the paper and then keep clicking on the pen until it says 'Help me'.
7 Put the paper into the cylinder.
8 Put the cylinder back into the pole and press the red button.
9 Wait for the cylinder to come back then take the paper back out.
10 Make a 180-degree turn to face the picture.
11 Click on the upper right corner of the frame, then click on the upper left corner.
12 Now click on the lower right corner and take the money.
13 Click on the money and then the pen. Draw a face.
14 Next put the money into the cylinder.
15 Go to the phone and dial 4357*63.
16 A deep voice will say 'OK'.
17 Go to the pole and put the cylinder back inside.
18 Press the red button and wait for the key.
19 Use the key on the door.
20 Congratulations – you have finished!

www.fasco-csc.com/works/bluechamber

Play on

You can ask the learners to imagine they are the person involved in the game and to write a first-person account of what happened to them.

Jumble jigsaw

Sequencing a jumbled text

The aim of the game
To put a walkthrough in order – by looking at linguistic clues – and play the game

Prepare to play

Find a short 'escape the room' game and look for the walkthrough. Add sequencers, as appropriate, and change the difficulty of the language to suit the level of the learners.

Separate each stage of the walkthrough into sections and re-order it randomly, as in our example opposite (adapted for upper-intermediate learners). Make sure there are enough copies for each pair of learners.

Play

- Before playing the game, the learners look at the jumbled walkthrough and try to work out the order of some of the sentences. Tell them that some of the words or expressions can help them decide which of the sentences come first – but don't be more specific.

- Sitting in pairs at their computers, one learner plays the game while the other has the jumbled text and tries to guide the person playing.

- As they play the game, the learners order the walkthrough and look for clues in the text to help them continue.

- After every three walkthrough sections have been ordered, the learners exchange roles.

- Once the game has finished and you are back in class formation, look at the walkthrough again together.

- Ask the learners to notice any language that helps us to put the instructions jigsaw in order. For example:
  - Sequencers (*first of all*, *again*, *finally*, *at the end* …)
  - Other clues – such as the indefinite article or the definite article (when you have come across an object before)

Play on

As a follow-up, you can select a similar game and ask the learners to complete the game for homework, writing their own walkthroughs and then mixing the instructions up to give to another learner to play.

The Bonte Room 2	Order
a) Use the ruler to stop the blades of the fan and get a chip card.	
b) Remove the metal grid of the fan once you've removed the screws.	
c) At the end, feed the parrot with the cactus-flavoured roasted peanuts.	
d) Finally, press the second rectangular button, followed by the red button and then press the first rectangular button and the fire will light.	
e) First of all, walk left and you'll find a coin on the top of the bottom picture of a bird.	
f) Go to the fireplace and notice the red button on the left and three rectangular buttons on the right (1 to 3 – from left to right).	
g) Get a ruler from the blackboard.	
h) To turn on the fireplace, press button 1, then 2, and then press the red button.	
i) Use the ruler to reach into the niche of the fireplace to get a wire.	
j) After the red button, press button 3, which will turn white. Then press the red button again.	
k) Use the sharpened wire on the cactus to make a puddle of cactus milk.	
l) Put the metal grid in the fireplace just above the flames.	
m) Put the wire into the blades of the fan to slice it and get a sharp point on the wire.	
n) Place the cactus-flavoured nuts in the fire and then take back the roasted nuts.	
o) Put the chip card into the slot of the peanut machine to get some peanuts.	
p) Place the peanuts on the puddle of cactus milk and then get cactus-flavoured nuts.	
q) Use the shiny coin to remove the screws on the fan on the wall next to the cactus.	

http://home.scarlet.be/~bbonte/bonteroom2.html

The order is: e, g, i, q, b, m, a, o, k, p, f, h, j, d, l, n, c

Tell me what happened

Police interviews

The aim of the game
To play a game on the computers first
and follow up with a roleplay

L S R W

Prepare to play

Choose an 'escape the room' game that is short enough to finish in the time you have available with the computers (ie one that has few stages, such as *The Bonte Room*). Find the walkthrough of the game and print out a copy for yourself.

Play

● Sitting at their computers with the game open, tell the learners that they are to imagine themselves as the person who has just woken up to find themselves locked in the room. Tell them they have no memory of what happened, but that they start having flashes of how to escape the room.

● Read out the walkthrough clues in order, using phrases like these:
  - *You seem to remember …*
  - *Suddenly you realise …*
  - *For some reason, you know that …*

● Continue until the learners finish the game then give them the following instruction:
  - *Go to a neighbour's house and ring the police.*

● Back in class formation, tell the learners that they are going to take turns being interviewed by the police, who are looking for the person who kidnapped them and want any help that the learners can give them.

● Divide the learners into two groups, with half of them playing the police and the other half the victim who was trapped in the room featured in the game.

● Tell the police to work together and start brainstorming questions. Give them some examples:
  - *What is the last thing you remember before you woke up in the room?*
  - *What did you have to do to get out of the room?*
Meanwhile, ask the victims to write down notes of what happened in the game in the order that it happened.

● Let the police conduct the interviews and collect the evidence. They should take notes during the interview.

● Finally, the victims write an official statement to the police about what happened. The police write a report.

Play on

You can extend the activity by presenting the 'criminals' (ie a couple of learners) next class. These volunteers will have to claim they are innocent and work out their alibi between them. The other learners then interview the criminals separately, trying to find holes in their alibi.

At the end of the activity, you play the part of the judge and declare the criminals innocent or guilty, depending on the evidence presented by the police.

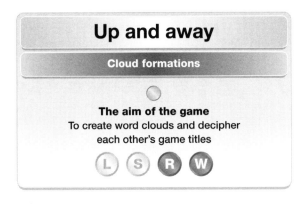

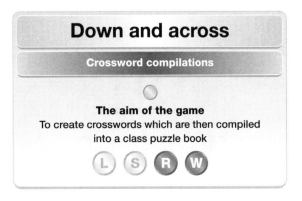

Prepare to play

Go to a website (*http://wordle.net* or *http://www.tagxedo.com*) that lets you make word clouds and create an example, inputting the titles of three computer games. The titles will need to be three words or more for this to work.

Play

- Show the learners your example and ask them to guess the three games.

- They now work in pairs on their computers and use the word cloud website to create a similar cloud with three different game titles.

- Ask everyone to stand and, working with the same partner, visit each of the computers and unravel the game titles in each word cloud. They should make a note of the titles, writing them down for later.

- Set a time limit of ten minutes and tell the learners the winning pairs will be those who manage to guess the most number of games in the time allotted.

- Stop the activity after ten minutes, check the answers and declare the winners.

- The learners can create a word cloud of *all* of the games (perhaps for homework). Decide on the best design and turn it into a poster to display in the classroom.

Play on

You can create another example using a song, or by writing a hidden message with a sentence of between six and ten words that reflects a structure from the coursebook.

The learners decipher it – then, working in pairs, they make their own word clouds, combining two sentences and playing with the design until they are happy. Finally, they invite the other learners to take turns visiting their screens and figuring out what the hidden messages say.

Prepare to play

Go to a site that lets you make simple crossword puzzles (*http://puzzlemaker.discoveryeducation.com*) and create an example crossword about a subject of your choice. Write the clues using relative clauses – in the form of 'A plumber who saves a princess' or 'A Facebook game where you grow crops', etc. Make a copy for each learner in your class.

Play

- Give the learners your crossword and ask them to complete it, using the clues.

- Ask them to choose a subject they are interested in (eg sports, the cinema, shopping) and to work in pairs, going to the website and creating a similar crossword.

- While they are writing their clues, monitor the language and help with any difficulties they may have.

- Now, if you have time, tell them to work together to make a list of 20 different words based on the subject of their crossword. For example, if their subject was 'sports' they could make a list of different sports, equipment, etc.
  - Tell them they are going to create a second crossword but, this time, the clues will be *anagrams* of the vocabulary they have just brainstormed.
  - Tell them they can go to an anagram maker site (eg *http://wordsmith.org/anagram*) to help them.

- When they have a list of anagrams, they can go back to the crossword site and make another puzzle with them.

- Finally, print out all the finished crosswords and collate them into a class crossword book.

Play on

You can give all the learners a copy of the crossword book to do the puzzles at home during the term.

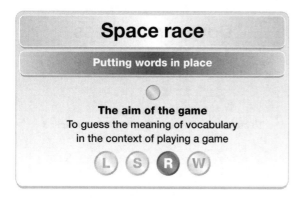

Space race

Putting words in place

The aim of the game
To guess the meaning of vocabulary
in the context of playing a game

(L) (S) (R) (W)

Prepare to play

Choose a game with a walkthrough and remove nine or ten of the key nouns (as in the example opposite). Make a copy for each learner.

Play

- Hand out your gap-fill text and ask the learners to read it and predict the words that are missing in each of the spaces. Encourage them to write down their predictions in pencil.
- Sitting at their computers, the learners then play the game, using the walkthrough.
- As they play, they identify the missing nouns from the text and fill in the spaces.
- The first learner to show you a correctly completed walkthrough is the winner of the race.
- Back in class formation, give feedback and compare the completed texts with your mastercopy, discussing any differences.

Play on

You can ask the learners to write their own walkthroughs for another game and take out nine or ten nouns, preparing it for the other learners to do.

The Thief 2 – Prison

1 Talk to the old man.
2 Give him a _____ .
3 Give him the _____ .
4 Talk to the old man again until conversation stops.
5 Take the spider's net from the _____ .
6 Go to the _____ .
7 Talk to the guard.
8 Pick up the _____ .
9 Take the bread.
10 Change the position of the _____ .
11 Talk to the guard.
12 Zoom in to the picture above the table and take the _____ .
13 Put this into the lock.
14 Talk to the guard.
15 Open the book.
16 Take the pencil and put it in the book.
17 Take the _____ and light it using the matchbox.
18 Talk to the guard.
19 Feed the mouse with _____ .
20 Talk to the guard.
21 Take the _____ and knife,
22 Cut the _____ with the knife.
23 Give some money to the guard.
24 You are free.

www.kongregate.com/games/Pastelgames/sneak-thief-2

Answers

2 matchbox	12 nail
3 cigarettes	17 candle
5 window	19 cheese
6 prison	21 bedclothes
8 cup	22 bedclothes
10 spoon	

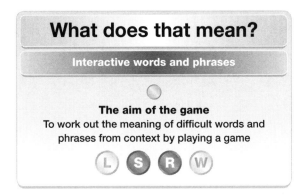

What does that mean?

Interactive words and phrases

The aim of the game
To work out the meaning of difficult words and
phrases from context by playing a game

Prepare to play

Choose a 'text adventure' or 'interactive fiction' game with
interesting vocabulary (one that works well with advanced
learners is our example *Spent*) and play the game. While you
are playing, take note of the most interesting/difficult words
and phrases and create a list similar to the one opposite.

Play

- Tell the learners what the game is about and then give
  them your list of words and phrases.

- Ask them to talk to each other and guess what the words
  mean and how they might occur in the game. Tell them
  not to worry about those they don't understand, but to
  move on to the next one.

- Stop them after five minutes and ask for some feedback.
  At this stage, don't explain the meaning of any of the
  words or phrases – tell the learners that you want them to
  guess the meaning from the context when they play the
  game.

- The learners then play the game in pairs and talk together
  to decide which choices to make. If they make the wrong
  choices and the game ends earlier than expected, ask
  them to start again and see if they can do better.

- After 15 minutes or so, stop everyone and go through
  the words and phrases again to check that they now
  understand them.

- If there is still vocabulary they are not sure about, ask
  them to use dictionaries to check the meaning, or help
  them by providing further examples.

Play on

You can ask the learners to write a narrative based on the
choices they made when they played the game and to use
some of the vocabulary from the list.

Spent

fast-paced   warehouse worker   take-home pay

opt-in   monthly premium   yard sale   curveball

lottery pool   fitness regime   keep you afloat

root canal   road-legal   pulled over   pitching in

landlord   loan   numbing gel   paid the price

expired registration   impounded   a physical

speeding   dent   bumper   tail-light   harangue

venting   IOU   paycheck   telltale   lets you go

http://playspent.org

Xpansion

I've got a little list

The aim of the game
To use a list of nouns to write instructions on how to complete a game

(L) (S) (R) **W**

Prepare to play

Choose a game that is difficult enough to require instructions to complete and print off a mastercopy of the walkthrough. Next, copy and paste the nouns from the walkthrough into a separate document, writing them down in sequence – see the boxes opposite, which use the game *Jobpico* as an example. Make copies of each for the learners.

Play

- Dictate your list of nouns out of sequence to the learners and cover any problems with meaning.

- Sitting at their computers, tell the learners they are going to play a game and then use the nouns to write instructions (the walkthrough) for someone on how to play.

- Put the learners into pairs to play the game and ask them to order the words as they appear in the game. They should write down notes next to the nouns (adding verbs, adjectives, etc) as they will need these later to write the walkthrough.

- The learners continue playing until the last pair has finished ordering the nouns.

- Back in class formation, they work in pairs to write a more complete walkthrough, expanding on the nouns.

- When they have finished, they compare their walkthrough with other pairs and with the printed mastercopy, deciding whose walkthrough is most similar to the original.

Play on

As a follow-up activity, the learners can write the walkthrough in the *past*, turning it into a narrative and adding descriptive detail as required.

Jobpico vocabulary (incomplete)

yellow cupboard   yellow towel   arcade game
desk   red chairs   memory card   chair
mobile phone   numbers   memory card   mobile
helicopter   red cloth   desk   blue object
puzzle box   squares   picture   web page
question   window   puzzle

Jobpico walkthrough (incomplete)

1 Look inside the second yellow cupboard to get the yellow towel that is there.

2 Move to the right and you'll see an arcade game. To the right of this, there's a desk with three red chairs. Look under the desk and you will find a memory card.

3 Find the mobile phone which is on one of the chairs.

4 Open up the mobile phone to see the numbers.

5 Insert the memory card in the slot in the top right of the mobile to control the helicopter.

6 Move the red cloth on top of the desk.

7 Click on the blue object inside to open up a puzzle box area.

8 Move the squares to make a picture, which will give you a web page to go to.

9 Remember the question written in red on the web page. Remember it because you have to type it into the window under the puzzle.

10 Go back and get the main helicopter part from under the puzzle box.

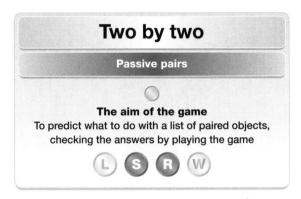

Two by two

Passive pairs

The aim of the game
To predict what to do with a list of paired objects,
checking the answers by playing the game

L S R W

Prepare to play

Choose an 'adventure' game and start playing it. As you play, make a note of what you do with the objects that appear in the game (or use the walkthrough to save time) and produce a list similar to the example opposite. Make a copy of the list for each learner.

You will also need online dictionaries.

Play

 Hand out your list of objects and tell the learners they are to guess how they are used together in the game.

● Ask the learners to talk together in groups of three and to use the online dictionaries to find out the meaning of the words they don't understand.

● After 15 minutes, stop them and ask them to tell you what they think the relationship is between each pair of objects in the game:
- *I think you use the hairpin to open the shed.*

● The learners play the game together. It should be easier to play because they know which objects they need to use together. However, if they get stuck, encourage them to read the game walkthrough to find out what to do next.

● Finally, once they have played the game (or part of a long game), ask the learners to look again at the pairs of words and to write about them. Encourage the use of the passive voice here:
- *The hairpin is used to open the shed.*

Play on

The learners can continue playing the game in their own time and finish off writing passive sentences about the objects.

Hetherdale

Look at these pairs of objects – there is a relationship between them. What do you think you have to do with them during the game?

hairpin & shed   claw hammer & canopy

magnesium flare & dark path

canopy & burning trunk   wheel chock & rope ladder

nails & planks of wood

chisel & wall   hand grenade & dam

winch chain & tombstone

engine oil & tombstone   steel rod & loose brick

plume & microscope

axe & reeds   guitar string & broken crossbow

make-up kit & statue

www.bubblebox.com/play/adventure/1747.htm

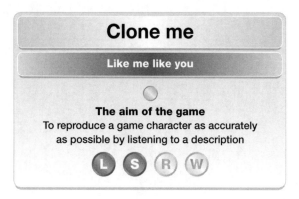

Clone me

Like me like you

The aim of the game
To reproduce a game character as accurately
as possible by listening to a description

L S R W

Prepare to play

Choose a 'dressing up' game such as *Hero Machine* that lets
you do more than just change the clothes (ie you can change
the way the character looks and manipulate accessories,
pets, etc). Create and print off a copy of a finished
character. Write a complete description of the character,
using language appropriate for your learners, as in the
example opposite.

Play

- With the learners at their computers and the website
  open, give them a quick glimpse of the character you
  have created and tell them they are going to try to
  recreate it (to 'clone' it) as best they can.

- Start describing the character and ask the learners to
  listen to you carefully. When you have finished describing
  your picture, they can start to create their character.

- Tell them to ask you questions about details they cannot
  remember:
  - *What's his hair like?*
  - *What colour coat is he wearing?*
  - *How many spots has the dog got?*

- When the learners have finished, read out the description
  again and ask them to check that their drawings are the
  same – or to change them.

- Finally, show the class the print-off of *your* finished
  character. Discuss which pair's character looks the most
  like it.

Play on

You can ask the learners to create a different character and
write their own description, using a copy of the written
description from the class as a model.

My Superhero

He's got spiky red hair, big blue eyes, big ears and a
mouth like a clown.

He's got a nose that looks like a cat's nose.

He's wearing a long green coat with a purple waistcoat
underneath and red trousers.

He's not wearing any shoes.

He's got a friend.

His friend is a dog called Spot.

His name is Spot because he's brown with two white
spots.

One spot is on his back and the other spot is over his
eye.

Spot is standing on two legs.

Dress up dictation

Recreating a character

The aim of the game
To listen to how an online character is dressed
and use a website to reproduce the image

Ⓛ Ⓢ Ⓡ Ⓦ

Prepare to play

Find an online 'dressing up' game – one that engages as many of your learners as possible. Make sure you will be able to direct them to the site quickly and easily in class. Play the game yourself and, when you have finished creating a character, write down a complete physical description. Take a screenshot of the finished character and print it off.

Play

◉ Stand pairs of learners back-to-back and ask them to describe what their partner is wearing, to warm up and revise some vocabulary.

◉ Sitting at their computers, direct the learners to the 'dressing up' website and let them play for a few minutes, so they understand how the game works.

◉ When they are all ready, dictate how *your* character looks – the learners have to listen and dress the character in the same way.

◉ The learners then stand up, look at other learners' characters, find differences and identify mistakes.

◉ Finally, show them the screenshot of *your* character and ask them to correct theirs.

Play on

For homework, you can ask them to use the same website, dress a character and write a description. In the next class, they exchange the written descriptions and dress up the characters by reading the descriptions

Coming soon!

Announcing a new game

The aim of the game
To create a poster for an invented game and then
present the game to the rest of the class

Ⓛ Ⓢ Ⓡ Ⓦ

Prepare to play

Choose a website (*http://www.glogster.com* is a good choice) that allows you to create an interesting poster. Alternatively, the learners can create a poster using word processing software.

Play

◉ Ask the learners to work in pairs and tell them they are going to produce a poster advertising a new game. This could be a new title of an existing game series or something totally new – the choice is theirs.

◉ To help them, you could give them the following chart and ask them to brainstorm the answers:

Title of the game:

Character names:

Place/setting:

Objective:

Obstacles:

Other information:

◉ Ask the learners to turn their answers into a poster, writing a brief description. Encourage them to find some images online to illustrate their ideas.

◉ Set a time limit (eg 20 minutes) and then ask each pair, in turn, to display their poster and give a mini-presentation about their new game.

Play on

The learners could go one step further and write the press release to the game, expanding on the text of the poster.

10 x 20 presentations

Presentations with a brief description

The aim of the game
To prepare and give a short presentation
about a favourite video game

Prepare to play

Short presentation formats such as *Pecha Kucha* (where you have 20 images and speak for 20 seconds per image) lend themselves well to the language classroom. This activity asks learners to present a game – speaking 20 seconds per image but only using 10 images.

The best way of showing the learners how to do this is for *you* to prepare and present one in class. Choose a game that you know and find ten screenshots of it for your presentation. Opposite is a possible structure that you and the learners may want to use.

Play

◉ Tell the learners you will give a short presentation of a game and that you will want them to do the same later.

◉ After you have given your presentation, tell the learners that they are going to do the same in pairs – they should find a partner who wants to speak about the same game as them.

◉ Sitting at their computers, they find the images related to the game they have chosen, while you encourage them to speak together to decide which ones to use. Alternatively, you can get them to do this at home and bring their images to the next class – or send them to you by email.

◉ Once they have the images, the learners can write out their presentations and rehearse them in class to make sure they speak for 20 seconds about each image. As they do so, monitor and correct their language, helping them with pronunciation.

◉ Set the presentations to change automatically (you can do this by changing the slideshow settings from *manual* to *auto*) every 20 seconds – the learners take turns to present them to the others.

Play on

The learners can turn the presentations into a multimedia slideshow, using Voicethread (*http://voicethread.com*).

Favourite video game presentation

1 Game poster/screenshot of packaging
2 Screenshot of main character
3 Screenshot of other game characters
4 Screenshot of space where game begins
5 Action shot 1
6 Action shot 2
7 Action shot 3
8 Action shot 4
9 Screenshot showing something unusual in the game
10 Last screenshot (show the game poster again?)

Prepare to play

Find an online image website such as *http://www.flickr.com*, which has a good collection of interesting pictures.

Play

- Tell the learners they are going to write a story based on a series of pictures.

- Ask them to work in pairs at their computers and find six images they like – and that they think are somehow connected – and to copy the pictures into a word processing document, deciding on an order for them.

- Ask the learners to discuss a possible story that links the photos and to write a word or phrase next to each picture. At this point, they can decide to change any of the images if it suits the story.

- When they have finally decided on their images, tell them they are now going to write a story, using the six images and expanding their words and phrases.
  - They can change the order of the images.
  - They should write two lines per image.
  - Each line should have approximately twelve words.

- Encourage them to discuss the story together before they write and help them with language as required.

- When they have finished, ask the learners to save and print their stories.

- Finally, display them in class on the walls (or using a data projector if you have a connected classroom) and ask each pair of learners to tell their stories in turn.

Play on

You can ask each pair of learners to take another pair's story and to continue it, saying what happened next.

Prepare to play

Find a 'point and click' game that takes place from start to finish on a single screen. Copy and paste a walkthrough into a Word document, play the game yourself using the walkthrough and then adapt the instructions using '*verbs + prepositions*' (verbs of movement). Make enough copies for each pair of learners in the class.

Play

- Ask the learners to read the walkthrough and discuss what the game looks like. Tell them that the whole game starts and finishes in a single screenshot.

- Tell them to use the clues they get from the walkthrough and to draw what they think the game looks like on a piece of paper.

- Take back the walkthrough and ask everyone to sit at their computer.

- The learners use their pictures to play the game.

- Back in class formation, they compare the pictures that they drew, and you ask them what they got right or wrong and what they need to correct.

Play on

You can ask the learners to make another drawing, but this time of one of their favourite games. Back in class formation, the learners describe the drawing to the others who have to guess what game it is. They can then show them their drawings.

Focus on the famous

An animated interview

The aim of the game
To create a dialogue featuring
an imaginary famous person

Comedy club

You must be joking!

The aim of the game
To make a short animated film
from jokes in English

Prepare to play

Choose an animated film site, such as *Moviemaker*, that is appropriate for the learners and for this activity (go to *http://www.dfilm.com*).

Play

- Brainstorm with your learners the reasons why some people become famous and how these people feel about being so well known.

- Tell the learners they are going to pretend to be famous, and put the following questions on the board:
    - *What are you famous for?*
    - *When did you become famous?*
    - *How did you become famous?*
    - *What do you like/not like about being famous?*

- Next, sitting at their computers, introduce the learners to the animated film site and tell them they are going to make a film of an interview between a TV journalist and the famous person they have just invented.

- Move around the learners, helping them with vocabulary and encouraging them to add details to make their dialogues more interesting.

- Make sure you leave time for the learners to watch each other's films and choose the best one. This can be done either at the end of the computer session – or later if you have a connected classroom (ie with access to a data projector and computer).

Play on

The learners can act out the interviews in front of the class during the next lesson.

Prepare to play

Find some websites with a selection of jokes suitable to the level of your learners and choose a few jokes with good punchlines (*Knock, Knock!* or *Waiter! Waiter!* or *Doctor! Doctor!* jokes work well).

Play

- Tell the learners your jokes and ask them which ones they think are amusing.
    - Do they know any jokes in English?
    - Do they think English humour is funny?

- Introduce the learners to the sites where you found your jokes and ask them to choose two or three jokes they like.

- Next, using *Go Animate* (*http://goanimate.com*) or another animated film site, the learners animate the jokes and prepare a short film to show the others.

- Once the filming has finished, organise a 'film festival' and hold a screening of all the films. You can ask the learners to vote for *best script*, *best film* and *best director* – as well as the funniest jokes.

Play on

You can ask the learners to select at random 20 items of vocabulary that they have recently seen (from their coursebooks, etc).

Armed with the list of words, they work in pairs and make a short animated film, incorporating as much of the vocabulary as they can into the story.

Set a time limit (eg 20 minutes) and monitor them as they create their films – if you see vocabulary that is being used incorrectly in a film, tell them where they are going wrong.

Face-to-face cartoon

Comic strip conversations

The aim of the game
To imagine a meeting between two people,
create a cartoon and then practise speaking it

Prepare to play

Choose a comic creation site. Although you can use most of these sites without preparation, the activity time is usually best spent if you *write* and *give* the instructions to the learners (see the example opposite). Directing learners in this way – and giving them a clear task – usually saves time and is more effective.

Play

- Go through the instructions with the learners and ask them to talk about the situation you have outlined (in the example, it is a meeting between two people who only know each other online).

- Ask the learners to say what they think will happen, and write examples on the board.

- Sitting at their computers, the learners go to the website and start creating their cartoons. Set a time limit (perhaps 15–20 minutes).

- Back in class formation – in a connected classroom or on the screen of the computer room (if appropriate) – play the cartoons and decide which one(s) you all like the best.

- Ask the learners to take turns, playing the part of some of the characters and reading the dialogues as the films are playing.

- If you like, hold a 'film festival', and award an Oscar to the *best film*, *best actor*, *best director*, etc.

- You can even ask the learners to prepare acceptance speeches (in case they win!).

Play on

You can ask the learners to write the story in reported form, using a number of different reporting verbs (*claim, wonder, protest*, etc.).

Face-to-face

The making of a movie

1 Start *Moviemaker* and select a 'Background' and 'Sky' from the list.

2 Press 'Next' and select 'Rendezvous' as your plot.

3 Press 'Next' and choose two characters.

4 Press 'Next' and write a 'question and answer' dialogue for the characters:
   - *Imagine the two people know each other online but have never met face-to-face.*
   - *What do you think will happen?*
   - *How will they react when they see each other?*

5 When you've finished, select the music from the 'Next' menu and click on 'Finish movie'.

6 Write the title of your movie (Face-to-face), add your name – and you can watch the film.

You can also send the film to your teacher and friends by email!

Example instructions for the comic site:
http://www.dvolver.com

Games on the move

If you want my opinion ...

The aim of the game
To write a review of a game a partner
has on their mobile phone

(L) (S) (R) (W)

Prepare to play

Make sure you ask the learners to bring their mobile phones
to class – you can also ask them to come ready to talk about
a game they have on their phone.

Play

- Ask the learners to work in small groups, making sure
  that at least a couple of people in each group have a
  mobile phone with a game on it.

- Tell each of the learners with mobile phones to show and
  to talk about a game they have on their mobile and to say
  what they like/don't like about it. Set a time limit for this
  of about ten minutes.

- Next, sitting at their computers, ask the learners to work
  in pairs and to write a review for a magazine of one of
  the games they have seen and heard someone talk about.
  Monitor this activity and help the learners with language.

- Ask any pair of learners who finish first to write a few
  lines of introduction to the magazine's 'mobile games
  survey'.

- After class, you can combine the articles into one
  document, add an introduction and print it out for
  everyone to read.

Play on

You can ask the learners to choose another game but, this
time, one they don't like – and to write a review of this for
the magazine.

Mobile merging

Proposing a product

The aim of the game
To combine two mobile phone games,
using images to make a new game

(L) (S) (R) (W)

Prepare to play

Make sure your learners all have mobile phones before you
do this activity. Ask them to come to class ready to use them
– but don't tell them what they'll be doing.

Play

- Ask the learners to turn on their mobile phones and to
  show each other some of the games they have. After a
  minute or so, ask them to change partners and to do
  the same. Continue for five or six minutes, or until the
  learners have spoken to five or more people.

- Next, sitting at their computers, tell the learners they are
  going to design a new game, taking some of the ideas
  from two or three of the games they have seen or others
  they know, to make a proposal for an entirely new game –
  a 'product sheet'.
  - They are to work in pairs.
  - They should write the title of the new game and a
    description of how it works.
  - They can also illustrate their 'product sheets' with
    images if they like.

- As the learners discuss what the game is going to be like,
  monitor and help with language.

- When they have finished, each pair of learners takes a
  turn to explain their game to another group. They then
  change groups until they have heard about all the ideas
  for new games.

- End the activity by taking a class vote on the game
  everyone thinks is the best.

Play on

You can ask the learners to write a letter to a mobile games
company proposing the new game.

Digital Play has suggested many ways of engaging your learners by focusing on computer games to teach language skills. But what about *you*, the teacher? Can you also develop, becoming more effective in your teaching environment and also widening your own horizons? The answer is, yes you can.

21st century teaching

As technology has advanced, so has its application and use in the classroom. This has affected both what we teach and how we teach it. We frequently have audio recorders and players, televisions or computer screens, video or DVD players and even interactive whiteboards – not to mention the technology that our learners also bring with them, such as MP3 players, mobile phones, etc. Maybe we haven't used them all in our own classrooms, but the chances are that we will probably have used at least one of them.

As the technology becomes more commonplace, we are beginning to see not only new tools but also new ways of teaching emerge. And as the focus in the classroom involves more than just teacher/learner/coursebook, such issues as reviewing syllabus design, rethinking classroom management and sharing information are also adapting to the new context. Our tried and tested teaching is not being questioned – it is simply being applied to the 21st century.

21st century teachers

With the advent of greater connectivity through the internet, it is now possible for teachers not only to have access to a rich source of online material but also to have the opportunity to be part of a larger global online teaching community. By joining Communities of Practice it is possible to share help and develop knowledge and experience of digital play.

To better understand the pedagogy involved, a wide range of literature is currently being published. Many of these books chart a rise in new applications of technology in teaching and explain how best to use these new resources to maximise learning and make the learning experience more effective. And who knows? Your own commitment to being a 21st century teacher might lead you to consider designing your own digital play materials.

In Part C, we look at ways for you to integrate your digital teaching within the school system and further your expertise beyond the classroom. Our suggestions, therefore, range from researching and recording online materials, both for yourself and for the larger community of teachers, through to producing your own games.

21st century teaching

From syllabus to set-up

Many readers of *Digital Play* may already have experimented with some of the activities in Part B. Perhaps it is time to move on – to incorporate games into your teaching 'system'. Games need 'game plans' to be successful in the language classroom, but they also need 'planning' in the wider sense of the word.

Let us first look at how digital play activities can be brought into line with the syllabus that you follow. From there, it will be useful to see how resources such as the ones that *you* use can be broadened out to include the *staffroom* where you plan and organise your lessons – in short, your colleagues, your school. And finally, we can examine some of the practical implications of setting up a 'digital play friendly' environment for the 21st century.

Syllabus

Whether you follow a coursebook, a national syllabus or one designed by the organisation that you work for, you will want to start integrating you digital play activities. You can start by matching an activity from Part B of *Digital Play* with one of your next classes – then begin to think more long-term by looking at your syllabus as a whole. Matching digital play activities in advance not only helps you to plan ahead, but also helps you to start thinking about how to adapt them: familiarity with the syllabus means that you can keep an eye open for activities and bookmark them for a 'syllabus fit'. How you actually exploit a particular activity in a particular class is your decision.

Activities

The best way to find digital play activities (apart from those you will have found in Part B of this book!) is to look online and start researching. You may find that compiling materials and activities will never have been so much fun. Here are two suggestions to help you find those activities:

- You can use a free online content monitoring service such as Google Alerts (*http://www.google.com/alerts*) or Yotify (*http://www.yotify.com*) to receive email notifications as key areas of interest appear online. You can specify key words, such as the name of a gaming genre, to better refine and restrict your updates from such a service.
- You can surf popular websites that you have identified as having appropriate and usable content. Such websites could be ones with an archive of online video games (a gamers' website) or any website that has got interactive and interesting content (for example, a TV channel web page).

We have seen how 'point and click' games are great to use in open class, or with learners working more intensely in pairs on computers. When used in conjunction with an adapted walkthrough, you can practise writing, reading and listening (for example, a live listening). Of course, digital play isn't just video games. Play can include a lot of fun activities, such as crosswords or word searches, designing comic books or creating mini-films or cartoons. To find these more conveniently, use key words in an online search engine. Terms such as 'creator' or 'generator', used after such activities, helped us find a lot of online interactive material. Why not give it a try yourself?

It is vital to make sure that any online material that you intend to use with your learners in a connected classroom can be accessed on the classroom computer/s and not just on your computer at home or in the staffroom. There is nothing more frustrating than finding that the *Flash* program needed to play a lot of games hasn't been downloaded, or that the connection is too slow (which is possible when the web page is being accessed by lots of learners at the same time). You also have to beware of web pages that contain inappropriate images or links to other sites which may, in turn, have inappropriate content. And sometimes, when looking at online activities during the planning stage, it can be easy to miss other content on the web pages, especially around the edges of the screen.

Language

What about the *language* content? It may not be obvious at first whether a game is best for grammar, vocabulary or skills practice. A lot of the material in Part B was not *designed* to teach or practise English, and so it is important to uncover the language *within*.

As you become more familiar with digital play and start to assess material critically, you will begin to notice language opportunities. Indeed, certain language items will be seen to occur more and more often.

- With a lot of online digital play, the action of clicking the mouse on an area of the screen produces a result.
- This is an ideal opportunity for either the zero conditional (What happens if I click here?) or the first conditional (What will happen if I click here?).

It is these opportunities that you will need to be aware of – and take advantage of at an appropriate moment in your syllabus.

Grammar

Uncovering the grammar within a game may prove challenging. Generally, it is the teacher who 'scaffolds' the grammar tasks. Firstly, we have to find a fun digital play activity that contains the grammar we want to focus on. We have to remember that, for a learner, it is the play and having fun that is the priority – for the teacher, it is the language and the grammar. Secondly, we should decide on a pre-game stage that prepares the learners for the activity and also introduces the play element. Finally, we produce material (a worksheet for an activity) that will lead the learner into the game with an acute awareness that there is also a language task to perform. For these reasons, both careful thought and preparation time are needed.

At first, then, identifying or uncovering grammar in digital play activities can be daunting, but it becomes easier with time and experience. Here are some grammar areas and ideas that you can apply to a wide range of online material – and some advice on how to focus on them:

- Conditionals – describing what happens in a game if you perform one action or another; predicting what will happen if you carry out various actions; visualising what would happen … ; imagining what would have happened … .
- Past tenses – writing what happened in a game as a narrative story.
- Present tenses – narrating live what is happening in a game.
- Future tenses – predicting what will/is going to happen from still images.
- Relative clauses – expanding on a walkthrough text, after having played the game.
- Adverbs – describing how characters perform actions in a game.
- Adjectives – adding details to objects in a game.
- Direct speech – writing a dialogue between game characters for a roleplay.
- Prepositions – using 'action verb + preposition' to describe a route in a game.

As you teach – and play – your list will become more exhaustive, and more specific.

◯ Vocabulary

Digital play activities can be used highly effectively to introduce, practise or recycle vocabulary items. Again, the teacher needs to scaffold the vocabulary tasks. And again, as a first step we have to find a fun digital play activity that has the vocabulary we want to focus on. Many online games or activities are topic-based and contain vocabulary sets:

- 'Escape the room' games can be used to spotlight household vocabulary.
- 'Dress up' games can concentrate on colours and parts of the body – as well as clothes.
- 'Simulation' games that raise awareness of issues can be used as a platform for discussing natural disasters or humanitarian issues – along with the corresponding lexical fields.
- Crossword generators can be used for students to compile their own fun tests.
- Creating an online comic or movie can involve the task of including specific target language.

In short, your learners can be given free rein to play a game that includes a list of vocabulary items that you prescribe.

Remember

Once you have begun to fit your store of digital play materials to your syllabus, don't keep them to yourself. The next step is to share them. The advantage of filing your materials on a network computer system at work is that they are kept exclusively for the use of teachers who work with you and have access to this network.

School

In our experience, once you have got teachers to start using digital play they begin to see the merits of its use as a pedagogically sound way to engage their learners in language skills practice. When this starts to happen you will find that not only does teacher demand for such activities increase but your colleagues will also begin to tell *you* about interesting websites, materials and ways to use them. It is now time, therefore, to start encouraging a more co-operative and organised approach to matching, recording and tagging activities.

For some teachers, a 'syllabus fit' is the best way to organise digital play activities. In Part B of this book, we concentrate on language skills and specify the equipment (no computers, connected classroom, multiple computers) but if you decide to match the activities to specific games, you may want to record and tag 'learner level' and 'language' (eg grammar/topic/lexical set) too.

Matching Once you have become built up a reasonable archive of digital play activities, and have begun to match them to your teaching syllabus, how you record this is up to you.

- A note written in a coursebook or equivalent can help to remind you there is a digital play activity and material that can be used to support or enhance the book: that the activity and material can be easily found and accessed in the classroom on the computer network or online.
- Sometimes, re-finding a game, interactive activity, video or still images can be as easy as typing a few words into a search engine and pressing 'Return'.

21st century teaching
From syllabus to set-up

Don't forget that you also need to be able to tell your learners clearly and concisely what they have to do both with the language and the technology in use.

Recording You can also record digital play files on network computers, as we have mentioned, providing the activities and materials with hyperlinks to web addresses by embedding them in a Word document and then storing them on your network.

- Being able to access Word documents created in a staffroom and then, later, being able to access them in the classroom or computer room is extremely convenient.
- It means that you, other teachers and learners can access a lesson plan, read instructions, look at material and go directly to activities.

Remember that in a computer room you are directing learners to a particular game on a specific website while also asking them to perform a language task. In our experience, giving clear instructions on paper or electronically can save time and cause less confusion.

Tagging There is, of course, the option of posting the same material on a blog or wiki as part of your professional development outside the school and inviting a wider audience to view, use and contribute to it. If this is the direction you would like to move in, then tagging your materials appropriately is vital. 'Tags' are labels assigned to the content on a web page to make finding and retrieving it easier.

We would recommend that, in addition to the considerations listed earlier (skills, level, language, space, classroom or computer room, etc) you may also want to include tags that refer to the title of the game, the genre (puzzle, escape the room, etc) and the source of the material (website, etc).

But the mere sharing of files, however useful, is not sufficient. We also need to invest in our own and our colleagues' development.

Developing Training within an organisation can do so much to help teachers take advantage of emerging learning technologies and discover how best to use them for digital play. Training sessions can take many different forms and could be organised by your school or university, or the initiative could come from yourself and your colleagues.

If there is a person who has experience and knowledge of a particular area, then they could perhaps be persuaded to give a workshop or talk.

- You could invite someone from outside to speak.
- You could share what a group of you are doing inside the school by organising a show-and-tell session.

If you know that a number of colleagues are interested in learning more, creating a small development group specialised in digital play could be the way forward. You could agree to meet once or twice a month to share your experiences and set objectives (do some action research, try out a particular activity, etc) to then report back to the group.

Remember

You can do all of the above – using learning technology is no longer the exclusive domain of a small group of experts. With an increase in the use of 21st century technology domestically, both teachers and learners have access to a whole world of resources. Schools, too, are recognising that investment in key technology areas is essential if they are to retain their competitive edge, be able to project a modern technological image and attract learners whose use of new technology at home is becoming part of normal everyday life.

21st century teaching
From syllabus to set-up

Computer management

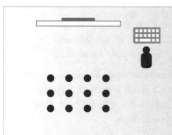

The teacher stands at the front and controls the information on the screen.

The learners are positioned (sitting or standing) focusing on the screen.

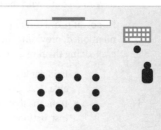

The teacher steps back from the computer and asks a learner to step up and take control.

The learners are positioned (sitting or standing) focusing on the screen.

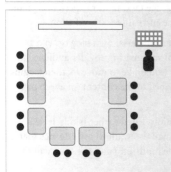

The teacher stands at the front and controls the information on the screen.

The learners sit where their focus can be drawn to the screen or a partner.

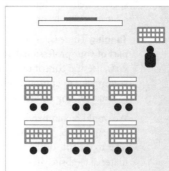

The teacher stands at the front and controls the information on the screen and monitors the learners.

The learners are seated in rows at their computers.

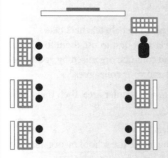

The learners focus on the screen at the front of the class. They then turn to their computers to perform a task.

The teacher stands at the front and controls the information on the screen.

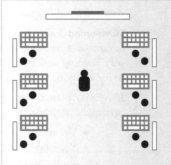

The learners sit in pairs or small groups and focus on the screens. Responsibility for control of the mouse, keyboard is allocated.

The teacher monitors.

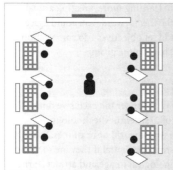

The learners sit in pairs or small groups and are focused at the screens. Responsibility for control of the mouse, keyboard and reading or writing is allocated.

The teacher monitors.

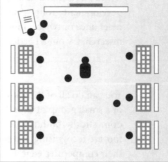

The learners sit in pairs or small groups. Instructions for the activity or a game walkthrough is stuck on the wall in an accessible location.

The teacher monitors.

21st century teaching
From syllabus to set-up

Set-up

Let us imagine, therefore, that the school has decided to invest in the technology and has requested your advice on how to make it work efficiently. What technology is required in a 'digital play friendly' classroom? As we have seen, the basic dichotomy of technology is: 'no connection' and 'connection' – whether single or multiple connections. In all cases, you can expand and improve the digital 'friendliness'.

No connection The absence of digital technology does not necessarily mean that there are no digital play resources. Many people forget that paper and print is a form of technology, albeit non-digital. Why not bring more of this 'technology' to your class by sourcing magazines, catalogues and books that cover a wide range of digital play topics and images.

- Magazines containing pictures or articles of computer games and consoles can be picked up from a local shop and make great realia.
- Material relating to technology can be collected and stored in a designated area in the classroom (for example a shelf, cupboard or box).

Digital technology can also be brought into the classroom by the learners. Why not start by asking them to switch their phones on? This is an unusual request, considering that learners are probably more used to being asked to put their mobiles away. However, a modern mobile phone can be a very useful tool – there will be content that can be used to generate discussion and dialogue (What games are there on it? How do you play them?) With a modern mobile, you also have at your fingertips a recording device or a camera (for both still images and video).

A single computer station You can recommend, and perhaps become the person responsible for, installing digital technology in the classroom, or even in the school. Many of the activities described in Part B simply use the following technology:

- The internet – a broadband connection with reasonable speed
- A single computer station – either a desktop or a laptop, placed centrally or at the front of the class

Investment in a projector is fundamental. When used with a whiteboard and with an internet-connected computer and positioned facing the front of the class, you can begin to present online images, videos, games and activities more easily to the learners. Classroom management becomes easier as learners do not have to be gathered closely around a single computer, and the need for an investment in multiple work stations is reduced. See page 102 opposite for illustrations of such a set-up.

Multiple computer stations If the school has the resources and space to include multiple computer stations, or a computer room, this can prove more 'language intensive' as learners move from an open-class focus to more pairwork-based activities.

Computer management and set-up are especially important when using computer-based activities with young learners.

- This is because the learners can easily become too distracted by both the media as well as the elements of play, rather than concentrating on the language task.
- Classroom layout allows us to establish a 'way to work' with the learners from the very beginning and orients them towards the task.

There is no doubt that a little law and order helps in the classroom.

21st century teaching
From syllabus to set-up

● A strategic and successful set-up

At this stage, you have to weigh the pros and cons of portable and fixed desktop computers. The former may prove more convenient and flexible, the latter have greater processing speed but are less flexible. Desktop computers cannot be moved around the classroom and, for this reason, consideration of their distribution is needed.

- Do you place them on tables around the walls of a computer room so that it is easier for you to monitor from the centre of the room? This frees up a lot of central space in the room which can facilitate easier movement by both teacher and learners.
- Do you place the computers on tables in rows? This more traditional classroom set-up means that the learners are still oriented towards the front of the class, which is useful if you are using a whiteboard or desk from the front of the room.

When you first walk into the classroom that we have just outlined, the first thing you notice is probably the tables, the chairs and, if you didn't arrive first, how the *learners* are seated. No doubt you are already familiar with a number of different ways to get your learners to sit and how important the layout of a classroom can be for an activity.

Having a clear idea of how to set up the layout of a classroom is very important for several reasons. One is that it manoeuvres the learners into starting positions in preparation for undertaking an activity. A second reason is that it lends form to the activity and makes proceedings flow better. To help you with this stage we included the diagrams on page 102 for you to consider when using digital play with your learners:

- If the learners are sitting in pairs facing the front of the class with pens and paper they expect to work together focusing on you or a board at the front.
- If they are huddled around a computer they have markedly different expectations.

When the multiple computers shown in the diagrams are placed against the wall, this allows for freedom of movement across the middle of the room. If your computers are set up differently (in several rows, for example) you will find you will have to adapt your own classroom management strategies accordingly:

- A greater overview of on-screen progress can be gained from standing towards the back of the classroom.
- Placing a walkthrough in a central position in the room will favour learners at the end of the rows. You should identify these areas and put the learners who need more assistance there.

Setting up the class in a clear, well-orchestrated and disciplined way also establishes you, the teacher, as the authority – this reduces behaviour and discipline problems. As you can see, your decisions can be crucial in the resulting efficiency of implementing the new technology.

> **Remember**

Finally, remember: technology enhances a classroom – it doesn't replace it. Making the most of the classroom is only part of the picture. The full picture is painted by you, the professional teacher.

And the more professional you are, the more you will be the one who is able to lead the way.

21st century teachers

From practice to production

There are so many ways in which, as teachers, we can take advantage of the internet in order to develop professionally. However, with so much on offer (and so much of it for free!), you may be asking yourself some of these questions:

- Where do I start?
- How can I get an overview of what is already being done?
- What digital play resources should I begin using – in my own teaching?
- How should I proceed – for my own professional development?

As initial steps, we would suggest taking advantage of the expertise of others to further your own pedagogical knowledge. Finally, you may want to take the plunge – as designer of your own digital games.

Practice

The 21st century answer is to join an edugaming-related Community of Practice (CoP for short), which is an informal group of practitioners (particularly online) who are interested in collectively learning and sharing information about a particular area of professional interest. Why get involved in a Community of Practice? It is an effective way to develop a resources bank, gain insight and get advice through sharing experiences, trading stories and exchanging anecdotes.

How can you find a CoP?

Facebook

This is the most well-known social networking site. You can either create your own group dedicated to 21st century teaching and invite others to join, or look for an existing group to connect to. It is another way to post links to resources, share ideas and generally network with a large audience of professionally-minded teachers. Here are four groups you might like to consider:

- **Digital Play** The *Digital Play* Facebook group regularly posts links to lesson plans, articles and videos, etc, from the authors' blog site *http://digitalplay.info/blog*. You interact with other group members, adding comments and starting discussion threads. It can be found here: *http://www.facebook.com/eltdigitalplay*

- **Hong Kong Digital Game-based Learning Association** This is a community of teachers whose aim is to provide a variety of education-based services that benefit learners, teaching professionals and parents alike. This group seeks to utilise digital games as effectively as possible to make formal education more fun and relevant to 21st century learners. Go to: *http://www.facebook.com/HKDGBLA*

- **Digital Game-based Learning** The stated purpose of this group is to promote digital game-based learning as a serious method of complementary instruction for use in educational environments. Its Facebook wall has a lot of links to news, videos and articles (*http://www.facebook.com/pages/Digital-Game-Based-Learning*).

- **Playpower** This organisation (*http://playpower.org*) provides affordable learning games worldwide, targeting those whose low earnings often mean that gaming is out of reach. Volunteers get the chance to provide input and direction on game design. Their Facebook page is: *http://www.facebook.com/pages/PLAYPOWER*

◯ Twitter

Using this social networking site (*http://www.twitter.com*) is a popular way of linking up with colleagues and finding like-minded people across the Web. You can use it to share interesting online tools and ideas as to how to use them in class, getting pointers, tips and suggestions from a wide range of fellow teachers internationally. We recommend downloading Tweetdeck (*http://www.tweetdeck.com*), which makes monitoring Twitter much easier. You will soon discover this is a time-saving way to fish for links, resources and information, and find people with similar interests.

◯ Google Alerts

Using an online search engine can often be frustrating and time-consuming, to say the least. Even when you know what you are looking for and your search terms are specific, the number of links that your search terms turn up can take a lot of time to look through and may be old news. When it comes to being a 21st century teacher, you want to be as up-to-date as possible. Using Google Alerts (*http://www.google.com/alerts*) you receive an email when something new is published online about a search term of your choice. The email will point to websites, news items, blogs, videos, discussion forums – literally anything new on the Web that mentions the term you specify. You can then decide if you want to follow the link and read more – or quickly delete it and move on.

◯ Social bookmarking

When you find a website you don't want to forget, you can always save it to your bookmarks or favourites on your computer. But a better way is to use a free social network bookmarking site such as Delicious (*http://www.delicious.com*) or Diigo (*http://www.diigo.com*).You can tag and save a bookmark online and access it on any computer, and also connect with other people and browse their bookmarks. Adding Delicious or Diigo to your browser's toolbar will make this easier.

Remember

You will get the most out of belonging to a Community of Practice if you are active, enthusiastic and professional. The way to go about this is to participate in the communities mentioned above, sharing ideas and responding to other members.

Pedagogy

Because *Digital Play* only scratches the surface of gaming in language learning and education ('edugaming'), and also because it is more practical than academic, you may want to read more in order to deepen your knowledge of the pedagogy involved. Here is a brief list of books that look at gaming and digital play as valuable teaching tools:

- **What Video Games Have to Teach Us about Learning and Literacy by James Paul Gee / Palgrave Macmillan 2003**
  This classic and thought-provoking book was ground-breaking in its approach to the use of gaming and education. Gee provides strong academic arguments that question fundamental beliefs and assumptions held about video games. The book is credited with not only affecting the assumptions of teachers, parents, policy-makers and journalists, but also with defining a new direction in education for

gaming. A highly influential work that identifies and focuses on 36 distinct, but interconnected, learning principles that now underpin the symbiosis between gaming and learning.

- ***Don't Bother Me Mom – I'm Learning***
  by Marc Prensky / Paragon House 2006
  This is a very readable and interesting book that focuses on convincing parents, teachers and educationalists of the benefits of using video games with the young 'digital native' generation. Full of anecdotes, studies and news stories, it aims to debunk the commonly-held belief that video games are harmful to children, arguing instead that they may, in fact, be key in teaching a multitude of skills necessary for a modern technological world. If you are looking for an impassioned argument to convince fellow teachers, parents or the school you work in of the benefits of adopting gaming as a learning tool, then look no further than this book.

- ***How Computer Games Help Children Learn***
  by David Williamson Shaffer / Palgrave Macmillan 2006
  This highly accessible and practical book was a breakthrough in the world of gaming and teaching. Based on over a decade of research into technology, game science and education, Shaffer expounds extremely sound pedagogical reasons for incorporating a range of computer-based simulation games in order to radically reform an outdated education system. In addition, the author provides detailed case studies of uses of computer games and simulations within education.

- ***Fun Inc***
  by Tom Chatfield / Virgin Books 2010
  Revealing and insightful, this book takes a look at the influence that gaming has had on science, culture, business and society. Chatfield not only provides a critical look at the impact of gaming on modern-day life, but also broadens the scope and looks beyond the horizon – helping us to better understand where the rise and advance in gaming is leading us. The book provides a very positive glimpse into a future where the potential of gaming will become more fully realised.

- ***Guinness Book of Gaming Records***
  BradyGames 2011
  This very informative and authoritative book not only provides facts about sales and the industry behind modern video games, but it also acts as a snapshot of today's most popular and influential video games, game characters and game genres. In addition, there are articles on consoles, game designers, game music and soundtracks, the world of professional gaming and world gaming events. This series of well-researched and user-friendly annuals is also very interesting for teachers to dip into and use for classroom reading activities.

- ***Reality is Broken***
  by Jane McGonigal / Johnathan Cape 2011
  Games designer Jane McGonigal offers her unique perspective on life and how we can work towards fixing the broken reality of today's world through the power of play. The book charts the author's personal journey from simple face-to-face social games to those which are more complex and reliant on technology. The one thing they all have in common is that they increase productivity and happiness. It is the author's belief that this is the way we can shape a better reality.

21st century teachers
From practice to production

Remember

As well as books, you can find online articles, interviews and papers published by these and other experts in the field of gaming and education. Effective techniques for searching the Web such as using .pdf or .edu at the end of your search engine term can be helpful when sourcing such material. The former will look for search results that are downloadable documents, and the latter for results within an educational organisation.

Production

Educational establishments around the world are beginning to see the potential of video gaming and are incorporating aspects of video game design into their curriculum.

Many summer camps in the United States and Canada are moving forward and have started their own digital play initiatives. Signing up for 'tech camps' is becoming more common, and is proving to be extremely popular. In these camps, members can participate in numerous workshops that break down the process of video game-making into different components. They start by looking more closely at the distinct design principles involved in a host of different game genres. Sessions may also cover some programming and learning how to create animations as well as using computer software to create your own unique look and feel for a video game. There are even sessions on composing digital music to provide the soundtrack. Here are some considerations if you want to give this a go:

Genres

When designing your own game, the first thing you should decide is what type of video game you are going to create. Will it be a fast time-based arcade game with progressively more difficult stages? Maybe you'd prefer a video game with a stronger storyline, involving mystery, danger and intrigue? Or perhaps a puzzle game where logic and problem-solving abilities are put to the test? Whatever you choose, it's worth bearing in mind that the most popular games are roleplaying games and action games. The key, though, is to choose a genre which you have a lot of experience playing and that you enjoy. Let's look at some of the options that are available online for the budding video game designer.

Animations

Software exists that is designed to make it as easy as possible for the people who use it to develop their own computer games. It is designed so that you don't need to have in-depth knowledge or any experience with computer programming to use it. Just a few examples:

- **Game Maker** (*http://www.yoyogames.com/gamemaker*) is free online game making software that is quick to download and easy to use. You simply custom-make your own game by selecting backgrounds, animated graphics, music and sound effects, as well as the actions for each part of the game. This is a great way to make arcade games or a classic platform game.

- **Alice** (*http://alice.org*) is a free program which can be used to design and create games in 3D. There is also instructional material to support both teachers and learners and its online community has forums where people share their knowledge. Some secondary schools in the UK have started to use this in subjects such as geography and computer science.

- **3D GameStudio** (*http://www.3dgamestudio.com*) is an option if you are looking for a video game maker that is a little more professional – but you need to be prepared to pay a little extra. It allows you to build games whose graphics are on a par with many of the best-selling high-street console games, yet it is designed for use on a PC. It's worth investigating, especially if your school is interested in investing time and financial resources in video gaming.

- **StencylWorks** (*http://www.stencyl.com*) allows you to make your own basic shooter and RPG games. Unfortunately, the resulting games tend to be very basic (you can shoot or jump on an enemy to kill them). For this reason, this software should be considered more of a platform in which to look at the *process* of game design rather than a product. That is, you won't get very much mileage out of playing the game for academic purposes – but the road by which you arrived at the finished product may have been enriching.

- **Adobe Flash Professional** (*http://www.adobe.com/products/flash.html*) allows you to build your own interactive game content. Learners can produce both the visual and audio content and then create animated and interactive games. Özge Karaoğlu and Demet Küyükon have done this successfully for an English teaching project for very young learners, called 'Bubble and Pebble'. You can read about it here: *www.medea-awards.com/past-awards/2010*

Music

How many of your learners are also learning to play a musical instrument? You may be surprised to find that you have a few budding musicians in your class who are only too pleased to turn their skills to being part of making the soundtrack to a video game.

For the musically talented, a creative project which leads to producing a video game soundtrack could be extremely rewarding. If this is the case, producing the music live, using the right recording and editing software before finally producing a soundtrack, may prove a worthwhile project. Programs such as Audacity (*http://audacity.sourceforge.net*) or Wavosaur (*http://www.wavosaur.com*) allow you to record and edit – as well as cut and paste your own music. This audio editing software can be downloaded for free online. There may even be audio editing software pre-installed on your computer.

Programming

Video game programming includes scripting, level design, tool programming and gameplay programming. It is not for the faint hearted, and definitely not recommended for those who have not had some prior experience of programming.

- **Scripting** is a simple and flexible language that is created for a specific platform and so varies from one platform to another. On video game console platforms, scripting is used by players to create modifications (or 'mods', as the process is referred to in the gaming world) and customise their own versions of a game. In virtual worlds, scripting is used by participants to design their own in-world content and governs how objects behave and perform within the virtual world.

- **Level design** is more of a skill or discipline, and involves the creation of video game locales, stages and missions. A level designer is concerned with the lay-out of the video game environment, as well as its content. When the role of a video game designer is expanded to include a team, a high degree of co-operation, organisation and creativity is required. This is perhaps the most interesting aspect of programming for a language teacher because this process can be a great task-based learning activity.

- **Gameplay and Tool programming** are two distinct but inexorably connected disciplines, so we have put them together. They are both extremely technical aspects of game design and require a much deeper knowledge of technical skills.

  A gameplay programmer requires a talent for maths, traditional programming languages and an awareness of the instructions that are specific to the platform for which the video game is being developed.

  A tool programmer's expertise lies in designing and creating tools to allow scripters, level designers and gameplay programmers to manipulate the video game environment in which they are working.

If you do have a working knowledge of computer languages and wish to apply this knowledge to video gaming, then it is a good idea to look into getting a low-cost game engine such as Torque 3D Engine (*http://www.garagegames.com/products/torque-3d*) which uses scripting.

Remember

So, if you are looking for a long-term digital play project, then game design offers an interesting route both for you *and* your learners. You never know, one of your learners may be a budding gamer or games designer and you could be opening *their* eyes to the educational possibilities in gaming.

And you?

You yourself have just taken a step forward into the 21st century. Who knows where that may lead?

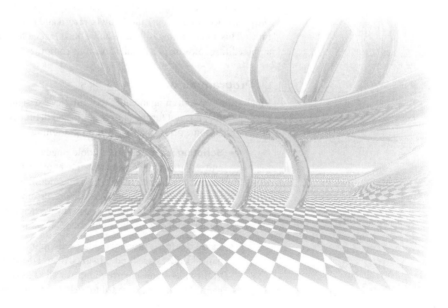

From the editors

Digital Play is a pioneering book on the use of computer games in language teaching.

Kyle Mawer and Graham Stanley are experts in teaching with technology and training teachers in innovative classroom practice. This book shares their excitement and their experience – through a combination of theory, practice and professional development.

- The authors examine the role of computer games in society, in education in general and in language teaching in particular.
- They dismiss stereotypes and review the latest pedagogy in implementing gaming with language learners.

- A bank of activities shows how to use digital play in the classroom, with step-by-step instructions that explain how to prepare to play, how to play and how to carry on playing – and learning – when the game is over.
- All the activities have a common aim: to help learners improve their knowledge and use of the foreign language, covering all four language skills through carefully drawn-up 'game plans'.

- The authors show the teacher how to integrate digital play activities into the wider environment of the syllabus and the school.
- They suggest ways of developing both personally and professionally as teachers of the twenty-first century.

Digital Play takes on the challenge of the digital revolution and is an eye-opening journey for all those teachers who want to move with the times – and with their learners. The book recognises what the learners do *outside* the class and tells you how to bring the world of gaming *inside* the classroom.

Kyle and Graham have demonstrated that the pedagogy is here – why not use it?

Mike Burghall
Lindsay Clandfield

From the publisher

DELTA TEACHER DEVELOPMENT SERIES

A pioneering new series of books for English Language Teachers
with professional development in mind.

Digital Play
by Kyle Mawer and
Graham Stanley
ISBN 978-1-905085-33-0

Teaching Online
by Nicky Hockly with
Lindsay Clandfield
ISBN 978-1-905085-35-4

Teaching Unplugged
by Luke Meddings and
Scott Thornbury
ISBN 978-1-905085-19-4

The Developing Teacher
by Duncan Foord
ISBN 978-1-905085-22-4

The Business English Teacher
by Debbie Barton,
Jennifer Burkart and
Caireen Sever
ISBN 978-1-905085-34-7

Culture in our Classrooms
by Gill Johnson and
Mario Rinvolucri
ISBN 978-1-905085-21-7

Being Creative
by Chaz Pugliese
ISBN 978-1-905085-33-0

For details of these and future titles in the series,
please contact the publisher: *E-mail* info@deltapublishing.co.uk
Or visit the DTDS website at www.deltapublishing.co.uk/titles/methodology